American Carnage

American Carnage

An Officer's Duty to Warn

STEVE NOLAN

RAGGED SKY PRESS
PRINCETON, NEW JERSEY

Published by Ragged Sky Press
270 Griggs Drive
Princeton, NJ 08540
www.raggedsky.com

Text and cover design by Jean Foos

Front cover photo by Tasos Katopodis/Getty Images. President
Donald Trump kisses the flag of the United States of America
at the annual Conservative Political Action Conference (CPAC)
at Gaylord National Resort & Convention Center February 29,
2020 in National Harbor, Maryland.

Back cover photo: Major Steve Nolan outside a medical aid
station, FOB Sharana, 2007 (a Forward Operating Base in
Paktika Province, Afghanistan).

All Rights Reserved
ISBN: 978-1-93397440-8
Library of Congress Control Number: 2020940484
This book has been composed in FF Scala, OPTI Franklin
Gothic and Neue Haas Unica Pro
Printed on acid-free paper. ∞
Printed in the United States of America

This book is dedicated to all those who have given their lives for the sake of liberty, and to all those who willingly bore that same risk but were lucky enough to return home.

In Gratitude:

Thanks to Monica Borrin Flint for help with the initial draft.

Special thanks to my daughter, Nooriel Nolan, for her many suggestions and invaluable help editing re-writes.

And my deep-held gratitude daily to be able to share a life with my wife, Barbara, a lifetime social justice warrior.

CONTENTS

PROLOGUE

MANY CLINICIANS HAVE SPOKEN OUT or written about the mental health status of this president out of a "duty to warn." This phrase refers to the limits of confidentiality in situations where the client intends self-harm or harm to others. In those circumstances, it is understood that the responsibility to the greater good overrides client-therapist privilege. While not able to formally diagnose a non-patient, a clinician can, and should, warn others when they see imminent danger. The purpose of this book is likewise not to diagnose but to inform what a particular diagnosis looks like in a position of leadership (& in this case vast power).

Given the outpouring of American mental heath professionals who have spoken up regarding the mental status of this president, the American Psychiatric Association felt the need to remind clinicians of the Goldwater Rule, which states:

> ... it is unethical for psychiatrists to give a professional opinion about public figures whom they have not examined in person, and from whom they have not obtained consent to discuss their mental health in public statements. It is named after former U.S. Senator Barry Goldwater. The issue arose in 1964 when Fact magazine published the article "The Unconscious of a Conservative: A Special Issue on the Mind of Barry Goldwater." The magazine polled psychiatrists about US Senator Barry Goldwater and whether he was fit to be president. Goldwater sued the magazine's editors in Goldwater v. Ginzberg (July 1969) and won a settlement.

However, in THIS case the danger is so great that mental health professionals have felt strongly that obligation to warn (while refraining from diagnosing) because it is a public health and safety issue. We are experiencing one of the most critical moments in our nation's history and it is directly dependent on the mental health of the sitting president, whose impairments are doing demonstrable harm to our citizens, our democracy, and the world/planet. There is no clearer example of a "duty to warn" than this.

In June, 2019, I had a conversation with a U.S. Congressman trying to explain why it appeared that we had our first personality-disordered president. He said to me, "I think all politicians are Narcissistic Personality Disorders." He meant large ego, which is not mental impairment. This is the problem when a term like narcissism has a common lay meaning. I conceded that politicians, movie stars, pop stars, have larger-than-life personalities and we sometimes use pejorative labels like egomaniac, but this is not the same as mental illness. I explained to him that he and most politicians were capable of feeling sympathy and empathy, know truth from lies, understand right from wrong. This misconception, confusing a large ego with a very real and potentially dangerous pathology, is silencing those who need to speak out and threatening the checks and balances needed for the survival of the Republic.

Diagnostic and Statistical Manual of Mental Disorders (DSM) Criteria

Narcissistic Personality Disorder (NPD): A pervasive pattern of grandiosity (in fantasy or behavior), need for admiration, and lack of empathy, beginning by early adulthood and present in a variety of contexts, as indicated by the presence of at least 5 of the following 9 criteria:

- Has a grandiose sense of self-importance.
- A preoccupation with fantasies of unlimited success, power, brilliance, beauty, or ideal love.
- A belief that he or she is special and unique and can only be understood by, or should associate with, other special or high-status people or institutions.
- A need for excessive admiration.
- A sense of entitlement (i.e. unreasonable expectations of especially favorable treatment or automatic compliance with his or her expectations).
- Interpersonally exploitive behavior (i.e. the individual takes advantage of others to achieve his or her own ends).
- A lack of empathy (unwillingness to recognize or identify with the feelings and needs of others).
- Envy of others or a belief that others are envious of him or her.
- A demonstration of arrogant and haughty behaviors or attitudes.

Antisocial Personality Disorder: According to the DSM-5, there are four diagnostic criteria, of which Criterion A has seven sub-features.

A. Disregard for and violation of others' rights since age 15, as indicated by one of the seven sub-features:

- Failure to obey laws and norms by engaging in behavior which results in criminal arrest, or would warrant criminal arrest
- Lying, deception, and manipulation, for profit or self-amusement
- Impulsive behavior
- Irritability and aggression, manifested as frequently assaults others, or engages in fighting
- Blatantly disregards safety of self and others
- A pattern of irresponsibility
- Lack of remorse for actions (American Psychiatric Association, 2013)

B. The person is at least age 18

C. Conduct disorder was present by history before age 15

D. The antisocial behavior does not occur in the context of schizophrenia or bipolar disorder (American Psychiatric Association, 2013)

Personality Disorder, noun (psychiatry): a deeply ingrained pattern of behavior of a specified kind that deviates markedly from the norms of generally accepted behavior, typically apparent by the time of adolescence, and causing long-term difficulties in personal relationships or in functioning in society.

What could happen if a person who met all the criteria for narcissistic personality disorder and almost all the criteria for antisocial personality disorder were elected to the highest office?

All personality disorders have problems with object (people) relations—their traits inevitably cause conflict. It is a notable list that follows.

Fired

John Bolton, National Security Advisor
John Kelly, White House Chief of Staff
Mira Ricardel, Deputy National Security Advisor
Jeff Sessions, Attorney General
Nadia Schadlow, Deputy National Security Advisor
Tom Bossert, Homeland Security Advisor
Michael Anton, National Security Council
H. R. McMaster, National Security Advisor

David Shulkin, Secretary of Veterans Affairs
Rex Tillerson, Secretary of State
John McEntee, Personal aide to the President
Andrew McCabe, FBI Deputy Director
Steve Bannon, White House Chief Strategist
Ezra Cohen-Watnick, Senior Director of Intelligence (NSC)
Anthony Scaramucci, White House Communications Director
Reince Priebus, White House Chief of Staff
Derek Harvey, National Security Council Advisor
Rich Higgins, Strategic Planning Aide
James Comey, FBI Director
Michael Flynn, National Security Advisor
Sally Yates, U.S. Deputy Attorney General/Acting U.S.
   Attorney General

Resigned

Rick Perry, Secretary of Energy
Kevin McAleenan, Acting Director of Homeland Security
Dan Coats, Director of National Intelligence
Alexander Acosta, Secretary of Labor
Sarah Sanders, White House Press Secretary
Kirstjen Nielsen, Secretary of Homeland Security
Scott Gottlieb, FDA Commissioner
Bill Shine, Deputy Chief of Staff for Communications
Ryan Zinke, Secretary of the Interior
James Mattis, Secretary of Defense
Nikki Haley, U.S. Ambassador to the UN
Joe Hagin, Deputy Chief of Staff of Operations
Scott Pruitt, Environmental Protection Agency Administrator
Tom Homan, Director of ICE
Ty Cobb, White House Special Counsel
Hope Hicks, White House Communications Director
John Dowd, the President's lead lawyer
John Feeley, U.S. Ambassador to Panama
Gary Cohn, Chief Economic Advisor
Rachel Brand, Associate Attorney General
David Sorensen, White House Speechwriter
Rob Porter, White House Staff Secretary
Taylor Weyeneth, Deputy Chief of Staff, White House Office of
   National Drug Control

Brenda Fitzgerald, Director of the U.S. Centers for Disease Control and Prevention

Marc Short, Director of Legislative Affairs

Olarosa Manigault Newman, Assistant to the President

Dina Powell, Deputy National Security Advisor

Jeremy Katz, Deputy Director at the National Economic Council

George Sifikis, Assistant to the President

Tom Price, Health and Human Services Secretary

Keith Schiller, Director of Oval Office Operations

Carl Icahn, Special Advisor on Regulatory Reform

George Gigicos, White House Director of Scheduling and Advance

Sean Spicer, White House Press Secretary

Mark Corallo, Communications Strategist for president's legal team

Walter Shaub, Office of Government Ethics Director

Michael Dubke, White House Communications Director

Vivek Murthy, Surgeon General

K.T. McFarland, Deputy National Security Advisor

Katie Walsh, Deputy Chief of Staff

INTRODUCTION

Clinical Background & An Important Discovery

I STARTED MY MILITARY CAREER as a line officer in the Air Force assigned to Electronic Security Command at Elmendorf AFB, Anchorage, Alaska. It was there that the seeds were planted for what would become my military career in mental health, although my thinking at the time was quite the opposite. I had originally planned to finish my military service obligation, go into private practice and attach to one city, a place to put down roots professionally and raise a family. My father had been a career Air Force Officer after serving in the Army in WWII, and we moved frequently as a family due to his career.

I left the Air Force to earn my masters degree in clinical social work from Barry University in Miami, Florida. South Florida was home; my parents had retired in Naples, Florida, and I had done my undergraduate work at the University of Miami years before. I graduated from Barry in 1992 with my master's in social work (MSW). I completed two internships, one outpatient with Catholic Social Services Counseling Center and one inpatient with the David Lawrence Community Mental Health Center, both in Naples, Florida, where my wife, daughter and I had settled to be near family. During these two placements I received clinical experience to the full spectrum of mental illness among the patients served, including personality disorder pathology.

Subsequently, as planned, I went into private practice but surprised myself—I didn't like it. There were the typical foreseen challenges of building a new practice but something unforeseen revealed itself to me: I simply did not like being financially dependent on those that I was there to help. Thus the idea of military service re-entered my life. The Army was in need of mental health officers at that time, so I joined the Medical Service Corps.

I was assigned to the 4th Infantry Division, Fort Carson, Colorado Springs, Colorado. After two years of clinical supervision I earned my first of two licenses as a clinical social worker (LCSW); I was exposed to the full gamut of psychological problems in that assignment: mood disorders, anxiety disorders (including PTSD), marital conflict, psychosis, adjustment disorders and personality disorders. It was here that I had my first experiences of discharging from the Service individuals maladaptive to the military due to the characteristics of a malady that makes conformity to social norms and values practically impossible. In a military environment that is clearly a game-ender.

My next Army assignment was for the Army Prison at Fort Lewis, Tacoma, Washington (the military Regional Corrections Facility). I had 33 sex offenders on my personal caseload. There were rapists and pedophiles, violent offenders and less pathological prisoners such as those imprisoned for drug dealing. It was here that I learned something that I was not taught in graduate school—most sex offenders meet personality disorder criteria (although there are exceptions, as that term covers a broad spectrum). It makes sense because the character structure of most sex offenders is completely self-centered. They are driven to get their needs met; the feelings of empathy that keep most of us from harming others is exactly where their impairment lies.

The major lesson that I took away from my sex-offender treatment training was an understanding of the high recidivism rate amongst this group of offenders. For the rapists and child molesters, those who do the most harm (this includes almost all violent offenders), there was a preponderance of personality disorder traits not curable. Whether criminal offenders or a more law-abiding individual with personality disorder characteristics (such as Borderline Personality Disorder), they are still maladaptive to social norms, which is why the military has a separate psychiatric discharge. The military simply cannot have someone wearing the uniform of the United States of America who cannot conform to rules and regulations.

While people diagnosed with Borderline Personality Disorder are predominantly female, rarely involve violence toward others and can have extensive mental health histories, Antisocial and Narcissistic personalities, in stark contrast, are overwhelmingly male and highly destructive and predatory. They have the potential, through war crimes, to embarrass or significantly harm the larger objectives of the United States and our credibility worldwide.

A contempt for or disregard of the Geneva Conventions (the rules that apply only in times of armed conflict and seek to protect people who are not or are no longer taking part in hostilities; these include the sick and wounded of armed forces on the field) would be a large-scale example of what I am talking about, while spouse abuse and child abuse are the more likely incidents to reveal the maladaptive character structure. This does not mean that the military discharges all perpetrators of domestic violence. Some individuals respond to discipline/education and/or punishment, and stop committing offenses. Not all offenders are diagnostic or have to be discharged, only those incapable of change. Some are able to hide unchanged beliefs (they want a paycheck, higher rank, career) but the underlying character structure/belief system remains intact; it lingers, waiting for a later opportunity. Thus, someone who has no criminal record back home might commit a war atrocity in a combat zone. This is not to say that all criminal behavior has a mental health diagnosis, but rather that those who commit violent crime have a prevalence of personality disorder features.

The two most prominent personality disorders among males are Narcissistic and Antisocial. They are the most dangerous at home or abroad because they lack sympathy and empathy, they are pathological liars, and they struggle to distinguish right from wrong. They rarely have any mental health history because they are what is called ego syntonic—they feel normal. They do not seek treatment on their own. They almost always come to military mental health by way of a command-directed mental health evaluation because they have violated the law (the Uniform Code of Military Justice, UCMJ). They do not fit the medical model where symptoms are ego dystonic (ego alien). Symptoms are normally felt as alien (toothache, migraine, depression, etc.), prompting people to seek relief/treatment. The military, in its wisdom, many decades ago, instituted a separate psychiatric discharge for personality disorder (previously called character disorder) because anyone possessing it is unfit for duty and the military does not retain anyone on active duty who is not worldwide deployable for combat. Personnel who are not war-fit receive a medical waiver or a medical discharge.

Later in my career I again served as Chief of Mental Health for a military prison, the Navy Brig at Charleston, South Carolina, and saw the same pathology amongst violent criminals: the lack of sympathy, the lack of empathy, grossly changing the facts of their cases (not aware that I had a record of trial), their inability to distinguish a normal sense of right from wrong, a natural or casual resistance to reform. There are exceptions, individuals who do not appear to be likely candidates for rehabilitation but who do turn over a new leaf, so each case must be assessed individually. However, it is almost a fool-proof test—those who are rehabilitated are not in the category of a personality disorder and those who continue to offend, after discipline and punishment, meet this criterion.

I have served in many other assignments during my career in mental health: Keesler Medical Center, Biloxi, Mississippi (twice), the second time cut short by the devastation of Hurricane Katrina which temporarily closed the facility, Patrick Air Force Base, near Cape Canaveral, Florida. I had a three-year assignment in the United Kingdom where I was the Chief of Mental Health for two bases, Royal Air Force Base Croughton and RAF Fairford. I was Chief of Combat Stress for Paktika Province in Afghanistan in 2007, and the Chief of Mental Health at Robbins, AFB, near Macon, Georgia, where I ended my career. In all of my assignments I had to deal with personality disorders. Although they are always a small part of the duties of military mental health personnel, they are an important part because they threaten either an individual, spouse or child, or the morale and mission-effectiveness of a unit.

The end of my career was more heavily involved in combat stress and Post Traumatic Stress Disorder (PTSD); after I retired from the military, I ran a PTSD clinic (Vet Center) for five years for the Department of Veterans Affairs. That too revealed important clinical lessons on mental health backgrounds, family of origin issues, and the links to resiliency or maladaptive behavior. This included occasional presentations of personality disorder features.

I am proud of my clinical involvement over all of those years in assessing and recommending the disposition of cases with maladaptive behavior due to psychopathology, those who were incompatible with military service, and a threat to esprit de corps and an effective mission.

1

"WHEN YOU'RE A STAR
THEY JUST LET YOU DO IT.
YOU CAN DO ANYTHING"

ON FEBRUARY 29TH, IN NATIONAL HARBOR, Maryland, the President of the United States attended the 2020 Conservative Political Action Conference (CPAC). He strolled across the stage to the American flag, took it in his arms, gave it a squeeze, planted his lips on it and mugged for crowd approval. He mouthed the words, "I love you, baby."

In 30 years of service to my country I never witnessed anyone hug the flag. There is a United States Flag Code that establishes advisory rules for display and care of the national flag. We have military honor guards trained in the appropriate handling of the flag, and it is indeed viewed as an honor, by those in uniform, to post the colors. The flag is treated ceremoniously for retirements, burials and other solemn occasions. The flag is never to touch the ground and when it is worn out the flag is folded into a trident and burned with dignity and respect—it is never to be discarded as trash. It's not an object to be used for grandstanding or self-promotion. You don't prove allegiance by physical contact, you prove allegiance by selfless service to country.

My mother, Lt. Katherine Flynn (Nolan), earned five battle stars during WWII for her brave service as a heavy casualty field hospital nurse in the European Theater. She treated survivors of the massacre at Gardelegen and the Nazi Concentration Camp at Bergen Belsen. She loved the American flag. She put it out every morning and took it in every evening. It was done respectfully. There was something sacred about it. She had seen too many die defending it (the ideals for which America stands), she had seen it draped over too many caskets, including my father's.

If there is one visual, one symbol, that could summarize a reality TV star's presidency, if there is one act that could define the emotional deficits and limitless manipulation of the narcissistic personality, this is it. The first self-admitted sex offender to run for public office, grabbed the flag and used it for his own gratification.

2

HOW DID WE GET HERE?

I SERVED UNDER SIX PRESIDENTS: Jimmy Carter, Ronald Reagan, George H.W. Bush, Bill Clinton, George W. Bush, and Barack Obama, three Democrats and three Republicans. They were all fit for command. As an Afghanistan veteran I am angry and I am saddened by what is happening in my country, by what has happened even within my extended family: I feel a tremendous sense of frustration because of what I know both through my military career and through more than two decades as a mental health professional.

Scandal and illegality usually end political careers and rightfully so. We still seek people of high moral character as scout leaders, teachers, clergy, law enforcement officers, within the ranks of our armed forces. We teach and learn and believe that a society should be built on moral principles. And so we have rules, regulations, laws, and commandments, and various levels of punishment for violators. We teach our children these tenets in order to preserve our institutions, our government, even our nation.

At Senator John McCain's funeral the McCain family got it right. You don't let an abuser, a bully, a person who demeaned the deceased, attend the memorial service. That decision was a show of decency, strength, and common sense. The president gave a speech seven months later and spent a full five minutes jabbing at this American hero. He said, "I gave him the kind of funeral that he wanted, which as president I had to approve. I don't care about this, I didn't get a thank you. That's OK, we sent him on his way, but I wasn't a fan of John McCain." This whole interaction with workers at a tank factory in Lima, Ohio, was obscene. American presidents never disparage Purple Heart recipient war heroes. His speech, classical narcissism: bizarre, because there was no need to bring this up in the first place, and grossly dishonest ("I don't care about this..."); he cared enough about it to make it part of his speech. "I didn't get a thank you." Narcissists' feelings are not normal or appropriate to a given situation. They cannot sympathize or empathize, so he insulted John McCain's widow and children by telling these workers that he did not get a thank you from the family. This display, by itself, was proof of mental unfitness for command.

In the domestic violence field there is an old expression, "When someone shows you who they are, believe them." Our current leader has a long track record and it is incredibly consistent, indicative of a particular character structure. In 2005 he did an interview for a show called *Access Hollywood*. It is important to absorb the language caught on tape because it reveals so much about the character of the perpetrator. During the interview, he admits to sexual assault, actually worse, he brags about sexual assault.

Three days after the tape went viral in 2016 he had the opportunity to address the nation about this incident, during a national debate, and he referred to his language as locker room banter. Of course, "locker room banter," even at its worst, is still about consensual sex, not sexual assault. This answer was that of a sex offender—but the moderator, and the nation, let him get away with it.

We did a lot of foolish things: We threw caution to the wind during the 2016 election cycle. First, by including a non-politician with zero government experience amongst the ranks of those running for the presidency, and then by ignoring all the usual disqualifiers: adultery, fraud, abuse, and especially lying. We allowed the man who wouldn't even accept the citizenship of Barack Obama (the two-term sitting president in the most vetted job in the country), to seek and ultimately obtain, the highest leadership position in the world. We allowed the repetition of numerous lies and never held him accountable, didn't let this kill the deal. There were never thousands of Muslims in Jersey City cheering the collapse of the Twin Towers in New York on September 11th and General Pershing never executed 49 Muslim terrorists in the Philippines with bullets dipped in pig's blood. Those strategic and racist lies, used at his rallies, were an early warning sign ignored. These are important examples because they illustrate the way that truth itself became irrelevant. That put us on the verge of something totally new in American politics—a free pass to a candidate and subsequently to a president who has no allegiance to factual information.

What was maddening to mental health professionals was the fact that almost no one was reporting the only logical conclusion as to why this was happening. Why was this man immune to the scruples that prevent normal people from lying and constantly contradicting themselves in public, and why was the public willing to let him get away with this atypical behavior? Early indications seemed to suggest that much of the public thought the candidate was merely a buffoon, or deliberately "messing" with people; however, it was the beginning of something new—a public eager to make excuses for a politician rather than hold his feet to the fire of scrutiny. Many seemed to enjoy the irreverence, his acting outside the box, the use of colorful street language; it became a slogan: "He tells it like it is."

Mental health professionals were not amused; familiar from within the walls of our own offices, what we heard sounded like a particular psychological disorder, especially the extreme narcissistic features. Scores of clinicians from all over the country signed group letters warning about the candidate's mental insufficiencies. Twenty-seven psychiatrists and other mental health professionals published a book in 2017 out of what they felt was a duty to warn, a public health warning about someone who was mentally unfit for command. They labeled it for what it was—a "Dangerous Case."

The more we found out about the candidate, and later the president, the more he fit the narcissistic and antisocial character profile. In an interview in 1994 with *Lifestyles of the Rich and Famous*, that resurfaced, he was asked who his baby daughter took after. He said she had her mother's legs but it remained to be seen whether she would develop her large breasts. The answer was pathological, an early window into his thought processes. It was abnormal to the extreme to sexualize a one-year old, completely deviant, the exact type of thing that should sabotage a run for political office.

Fast-forward to 2005 and the *Access Hollywood* video and you perceive the same mindset. He is obsessed with objectifying females sexually. When he brags about grabbing women by the genitals without permission, he jokingly says he can't control himself, asks for a breath mint as he and the interviewer watch an attractive woman approaching. He says that sometimes he just starts kissing them because he can't wait (that's sexual assault). His reaction to the public disclosure of the tape was that of a sex offender—he doubled down and like most sex offenders was unaware that the failure to understand the gravity of the offense is one of the main features of character disorder (personality disorder). It is an inadvertent confession of wrongdoing. The specific language is important.

> *I did try and fuck her. She was married. I moved on her like a bitch, but I couldn't get there. And she was married. Then all of a sudden I see her, she's now got the big phony tits and everything. She's totally changed her look. I've gotta use Tic Tacs, just in case*

I start kissing her. You know I'm automatically attracted to beau-
tiful—I just start kissing them. It's like a magnet. Just kiss. I don't
even wait. And when you're a star, they let you do it. You can do
anything. Grab 'em by the pussy. You can do anything."

Fast-forward again to 2016 and the Commander-in-Chief forum with
Matt Lauer. The presidential candidate responds to a question about a
tweet concerning sexual assault of women in the military, "What did
these geniuses expect when they put men and women together?" I wrote
an Op-Ed piece in answer to that question. I wrote about what they
expected, what my mother, the WWII combat nurse, expected when
she enlisted in the Army: the privilege of serving her country alongside
her male colleagues and the undying gratitude of the men she helped
save. The point was the candidate's disconnect, what his thoughts and
words revealed on this subject—a complete lack of respect for women
and a belief that men cannot control themselves when put around them.
This mind-set leads to an abdication of responsibility, a vindication of
both himself and of men who abuse women. With that quote he sent a
clear message to every woman in military uniform—they would be less
protected under this Commander in Chief.

(And with this message, the soon-to-be 45th president, once again
revealed beliefs consistent with personality disorder pathology).

As I said in the introduction, my career spanned 30 years, most of
it as a military mental health officer. It was always part of my duties to
deal with personality disorders and implement the separate psychiatric discharge from military service for this particular pathology. These
individuals must be discharged because their beliefs and actions are not
compatible with military service; they are maladaptive, and the condition
is incurable. The two most dangerous conditions are antisocial personality disorder and narcissistic personality disorder because these are
the two most associated with victimizing others. We cannot afford to
send such individuals to a combat zone or we risk Geneva Conventions
violations. Anyone can Google the criteria for these disorders but, as I
mentioned in the prologue, an easy way to understand the symptoms in
such people is that they lack sympathy and empathy, they are habitual
liars and they don't favor right over wrong. It is easy to see how they
would cause mayhem. Habitual lying alone would end any military
career; but it is the lack of a moral compass, the absence of remorse/
regret, the lack of symptoms/suffering that marks this disorder (ego-syn-
tonic). These people feel normal to themselves, so they do not seek
treatment. They rarely have a mental health record.

Had I been faced with any service member who stated that sexual assault was due to putting men and women together, who refused to believe that their Commander in Chief was a U.S. citizen, who thought he knew more than the generals, who believed and claimed that enemy leadership was stronger than American leadership, that we should murder family members of terrorists, that the Geneva Conventions tie the hands of our military, that proven U.S. intelligence is a hoax, that Neo-Nazis are fine people, or that a free press is the enemy of the people, I would be obligated to discharge that person from the military.

These are all the un-recanted beliefs and public pronouncements of the current Commander in Chief. For the first time in American history we have someone in charge of the military who would be unfit to hold the lowest rank within the military.

3

"I'M A VERY STABLE GENIUS"

THE PRESIDENT OF THE UNITED STATES is never going to agree to a voluntary neuropsychiatric examination/psychosocial assessment to prove he is mentally fit for command, but it doesn't matter whether he is ever diagnosed. If I had a soldier/client on my caseload who raped another soldier and refused a psychiatric evaluation, it wouldn't change the reality of the situation or the necessary consequences. It is not just that the president meets all the criteria of a particular character profile, it's that every day, with his Twitter account alone, he confirms the cognitive and emotional problems associated with this disorder. Up to this point, cheating on a spouse, illegal payments to a porn star, running a fraudulent charity or a fraudulent university, would have rendered any previous candidate unelectable. The characteristics of a narcissist are incompatible with service to country. We have generals and admirals who live by a strict code of duty and honor and justice, whose careers would be over if they stole a pack of chewing gum from a convenience store. They are now working for someone who has paid a $25 million fine for defrauding students and a $2 million fine for defrauding contributors to his charity just since winning the presidential election. This is a formula for disaster. You cannot put people of honor under the leadership of someone with none. What is typical of the antisocial and narcissistic character structure is not only the ability to victimize others but a total lack of remorse. It does not help us as a nation that we are so used to the deceit of this individual that the victims (the students and charitable contributors) hardly make the news cycle as the most significant story.

Even in negative reporting about this president, the missing piece to the puzzle is the question WHY? Why is this president so different from anything we've seen before? For many people the answer is that he was never a politician, for others the answer is that he is a businessman or a reality TV star, and they seem satisfied with these explanations for the way he operates. For myself and clinicians nationwide the answer is quite different, and scary, because the lack of remorse and regret, the ability to be cruel, to break the law, to victimize others, to trash the checks and balances of our system of government, are all made possible by and indicative of a specific pathology. In the past three years we have been forced to witness our country, our allies, and inevitably Congress, through the impeachment, treat a clearly abnormal person as if he is mentally fit for command.

It is near impossible to convey the frustration of having to endure this presidency as a mental health professional and career military officer. Impeachment was predicted by almost all of my colleagues because the president's character profile lacks morality. We discharge people without morals because, if kept on active duty, disaster is inevitable.

The disaster we were anticipating occurred early. First came the lie that Iran violated a nuclear agreement. It was the consensus of our nuclear experts, our allies (Germany, France, Great Britain) as well as China and Russia that Iran had not violated the agreement. This was the first event affecting regional and national security that we, as a nation, allowed to be hushed into silence, permitted falsehood to negate truth, and altered foreign policy. The second incident that should also have been too big, too serious to allow to pass was the president's announcement, after one meeting with Kim Jong-un, that North Korea was no longer a nuclear threat. This too went mostly unchallenged, due to its absurdity, but it ushered in a very dangerous precedent: we were now going to allow the President of the United States to misinform the people about matters of critical importance. What went unexamined was the pathology behind it and the slow mission creep of the truth being replaced by "alternative facts," (that alternative reality introduced by the president's counselor, Kellyanne Conway, on NBC's *Meet the Press* on January 22, 2017.

Congress not only became more complicit; they allowed themselves to become increasingly irrelevant. The end goal of a narcissist is to spin every event to conform to their version of reality and have it accepted as fact. The president has continually repeated that anything printed against him is fake news, but he didn't stop there. He upped the ante to the unconstitutional declaration that "the press is the enemy of the people." This belief alone would eliminate any recruit from military service—the very military that the president commands. After this declaration from the White House, former President George W. Bush felt the need to speak out (*Today Show*, February 27,

2017) saying, "I consider the media to be indispensable to democracy, we need an independent media to hold people like me to account."

That rare act should have had a greater impact on the entire nation—a former president was countering a sitting president's statement and warning us that this belief is anti-democratic. Like President Bush, every member of Congress should have publicly condemned that assault on our Constitution, the Constitution they all took an oath to defend.

4

CAPITULATION TO AN ENEMY

How We Betrayed an American POW

ON JULY 16, 2018, IN HELSINKI, FINLAND, America witnessed an unprecedented spectacle—the Commander in Chief standing next to a dictator, Vladimir Putin, and telling the world that he had confidence in both parties, meaning in U.S. intelligence and in the enemy's denial of cyber warfare against the United States. Our president had already lobbied for Russian re-instatement into the G8 while we were still under attack by Vladimir Putin. I cannot overemphasize the clinical significance of this behavior.

(Robert Mueller, at the end of the Department of Justice investigation into Russian interference in the 2016 election, said that Russian cyber warfare was pervasive and that it had never stopped).

John McCain, having served and sacrificed for his country in heroic fashion, knew that what he was witnessing was dangerous, a national security threat. It was a disgraceful, mind-boggling performance. He said that the President of the United States went to Helsinki and abased himself in front of a tyrant; but I doubt that John McCain, like most of America, could fathom why.

We had already expelled 35 Russian spies, Congress had voted 317-5 to impose economic sanctions on Russia as punishment for its espionage and we were indicting 12 Russian Army Intelligence officers for their cyber warfare. There was overwhelming proof of Russian meddling by our intelligence community.

The president's performance was the equivalent of John Fitzgerald Kennedy saying that he had Khrushchev's word there were no missiles in Cuba (during the Cuban Missile crisis, October, 1962). It was an absolutely astounding declaration the likes of which I had never seen in my career (which started in Alaska, witnessing our electronic surveillance of the Soviets and vice versa). It was a betrayal of

America by the president. It was a betrayal of all those who had fought and died and endured imprisonment defending America and liberty.

The country should have reacted with horror. The president's actions were unprecedented but the question of why this president would suck up to an enemy dictator was never seriously addressed. However, it came as no surprise to the mental health community, that a pathological narcissist could have a personal agenda (even an anti-American agenda) take precedence over our national interests and safety.

The resignation of Secretary of Defense James Mattis was a warning that this president was turning the world order upside down; a world order that had provided peace and security for over 70 years. The Secretary's letter of resignation clearly stated the dangers of abandoning our allies and courting our enemies. But why this letter was necessary, the powerful message it was meant to convey, seemed lost. It was not helped by the fact that the president told the nation, and this is no small thing psychologically (actually huge diagnostically), that Secretary Mattis retired. Once again the president showed how comfortable he is in re-writing history. As he did in Helsinki, he demonstrated the one narcissistic quality that has the potential to destroy our nation when the perpetrator happens to be the President of the United States—the turning of fact to fiction. So dangerous is this symptom in any person with NPD, that he or she is discharged from the military upon diagnosis.

Many voices of reason and dissent have left this administration; Army and Marine Corps generals are gone—either fired or have resigned. All for the same reported reason: they bucked the personal agenda of the narcissist.

All presidents are, by design, subordinate to the Constitution. The only oath they take is to defend that founding document of our democracy. Thus, it was not surprising that an early resignation of this president's administration was Walter Shaub, Government Ethics Director, who simply could not tolerate the president's anti-constitutional behavior from day one, failing to divest from his companies and giving waivers to appointees to skirt ethics rules. Shaub was not willing to compromise his own integrity, his own duty and oath of office. We witnessed the same pattern with the whistleblower (who reported the president's conversation with the president of the Ukraine) and the members of the State Department and White House who testified in the impeachment hearings against improper behavior concerning Ukraine.

We are currently witnessing the same pattern with members of the medical community and federal health agencies during a pandemic—having to contradict the president for the sake of the greater public. And, once again, even though the nation is puzzled by the president's behavior, the idea that he is mentally unfit for the highest office has no traction. Invoking the 25th Amendment, the one immediate remedy, is not, to our knowledge, a pending consideration by leadership. I am convinced it is due to the fact that so few people know anything about personality disorder pathology and how to recognize it. In this case, one must assume that includes the Vice President and Cabinet who would be required to initiate the invocation.

The good news is that we may never have to face a similar situation again if the voting public returns to the previous requirement that a candidate for president be a person of honesty, integrity, courage, moral leadership and believe in the founding principles of our country. Let us examine the proof that this is not what happened during the election of 2016. Let me break it down clinically.

5

THE TWEETS

Unfiltered Evidence of His Beliefs, His State of Mind

10/11/17 *With all of the Fake News coming out of NBC and the Networks, at what point is it appropriate to challenge their license? Bad for country!*

Early on, the president clearly demonstrated his anti-American belief systems and his contempt for checks and balances on authority and on truth. He created a mantra that any information he didn't like was "fake news." His particular target for criticism is the "mainstream media," news organizations with an international reputation for fact checking such as the television networks, the *New York Times*, the *Washington Post*, the *Wall Street Journal*, the BBC, and CNN. Later he would label such organizations the "enemy of the people." In this tweet he suggests that perhaps this free press should lose their license. He plants the dangerous seed that the press is bad for the country. This is a sign of his megalomania, a toxic level of narcissism that assumes powers far beyond the presidency as we know it.

5/28/2018 *Happy Memorial Day! Those who died for our great country would be very happy and proud at how well our country is doing today. Best economy in decades, lowest unemployment numbers for blacks and Hispanics EVER (& women in 18 years), rebuilding our Military and so much more. Nice!*

The president was incapable of praising our military dead for their ultimate sacrifice. His tweet is all about himself, his programs, his economy. There has never been a president before who would think it proper to ignore our military dead on Memorial Day, or who would get away with doing so. What is particularly diagnostic is his capitalizing the word EVER. It is the definitive proof that his focus is on his own accomplishments, not the valor and bravery of our deceased heroes. This tweet is so abnormal that it amazed me that even amongst the civilian population this was not more of an outrage. For those of us who have family buried in Arlington, it was sacrilege.

2/18/19 *North Korea, under the leadership of Kim Jong-un, will become a great Economic Powerhouse. He may surprise some but he won't surprise me, because I have gotten to know him and fully understand how capable he is. North Korea will become a different kind of Rocket—an Economic one!*

How "capable" he is? Kim Jong-un was charged with crimes against humanity by the United Nations Commission in 2014. His atrocities include: indoctrination, prison gulags, executions, murder, forced abortions, religious persecutions and starvation. Any previous president would be incapable of praising someone who is one of the worst human rights violators on the planet. In fact, there would be no reason to have a military, no reason to go to war, no reason to have enemies, if these things did not matter. They do not sufficiently matter to the narcissist or antisocial personality disordered person. Everything is subordinate to immediate economic concerns (North Korea will become an economic rocket); the narcissist has a character structure dominated by self-centeredness and immediate gratification. Image is more important than substance. All deals, or even the appearance of a deal (North Korea, Ukraine) are structured to benefit the same one person, the president himself.

6/16/19 *A poll should be done on which is the more dishonest and deceitful newspaper, the Failing New York Times or the Amazon (lobbyist) Washington Post! They are both a disgrace to our country, the Enemy of the People, but just can't seem to figure out which is worse? The good...*

He calls two of America's most respected and awarded news outlets a disgrace to our country, a personal attack using deliberate language to eliminate sources of truth, eliminate opposition to an agenda defined by blatant lies. Even non-clinical people should have begun to realize that there was something seriously wrong with this thinking so clearly opposed to American values. After this tweet there should not have been a single supporter of the president left in Congress. It is so anti-American, a complete betrayal of the oath they all take. This declaration would have ended the military service of anyone in uniform, all of whom swear to defend the Constitution—it is a complete contradiction of that oath to believe that a free press is our enemy. There was a voice of reason in the Congress—Senator Jeff Flake warned in his retirement speech "you cannot accept what is clearly abnormal as the new normal." Senator Flake was not a clinician but he understood that something unprecedented and dangerous was happening.

6/16/19 *...news is that at the end of 6 years, after America has been made GREAT again and I leave the beautiful White House (do you think the people would demand that I stay longer? KEEP AMERICA GREAT), both of these horrible papers will quickly go out of business and be forever gone!*

Two very important and revealing things in this continued thought/tweet:

No other president has ventured into picking on any American business let alone tried to predict their future or relish their demise. This is abnormal. U.S. presidents believe in free enterprise, capitalism and the right of the marketplace to decide which businesses succeed or fail. Every president also believes in the will of the people to decide such economic outcomes as well as who sits in power in this country. But the president continues his onslaught of the *New York Times* and *Washington Post* because they are known for great journalism and allegiance to truth. They are associated with revelations about the Pentagon Papers and Watergate, a free press being essential to democracy.

What is more disturbing, more indicative of the pathological narcissism, is his reference to extending his presidency beyond current term limits. "Do you think the people would demand I stay longer?" He asks coyly and then he lets us know in capital letters that that's what would KEEP AMERICA GREAT. This declaration of a personal wish to remain in power, plants a seed in the minds of his supporters that is contrary to our democratic process.

7/2/19 *A very sad time for America when the Supreme Court of the United States won't allow a question of "is this person a citizen... (census)*

2/24/20 *"Sotomayor accuses GOP appointed Justices of being biased in favor of Trump." @ingrahamAngle@FoxNews This is a terrible thing to say. Trying to "shame" some into voting her way? She never criticized Justice Ginsberg when she called me a "faker." Both should recuse themselves...*

2/24/20 *...on all things Trump, or Trump related, matters! While "elections have consequences," I only ask for fairness, especially when it comes to decisions made by the United States Supreme Court!*

The Supreme Court is a co-equal branch of government yet the president claims it to be "sad" if the justices disagree with him. He says they "should" recuse themselves. He sits in judgment over them rather than accept their autonomy. His comments are an inadvertent admission that he does not accept our form of government of checks and balances. Previous presidents respected the legislative and judicial branches of our government and appreciated their place in the balance of power. To the narcissist, anything he cannot control or does not go his way seems wrong. The narcissist cannot appreciate the long-term implications, the long-term virtues (like freedom of the press) vital to preserving democracy. Anything that is a roadblock to their will is wrong. Again, one of the symptoms is the audacity to say these things out loud and see nothing wrong with them. What is unacceptable, and has created a much bigger problem, is that no members of his political party, with the exception of John McCain, Jeff Flake and Mitt Romney, publicly opposed this language and thinking, which go against the American constitution and are thus inherently anti-American.

7/08/19   *I have been very critical about the way the U.K. and Prime Minister Theresa May handled Brexit. What a mess, I told her how it should be done...*

It goes against the norms of international diplomacy for American presidents to criticize allied leaders publicly but this is more than criticism. There is the added narcissistic twist that the president told the prime minister how she should lead her own country.

7/15/19   *We will never be a Socialist or Communist Country. IF YOU ARE NOT HAPPY HERE YOU CAN LEAVE! ... Certain people hate our country.*

It defies all presidential norms to ask Americans to leave our country because of philosophical or political beliefs. We are all taught that basic American right: freedom of belief. When Ronald Reagan was asked during the McCarthy hearings whether he thought the Communist Party should be outlawed in America, he said that as a citizen he would not like to see any political party outlawed on the basis of political ideology; and that "he would not want to see us, so urged by fear or resentment of any party, compromise our democratic principles." The 45th president not only goes after people's free speech, he informs us what is in their hearts. No previous president in my lifetime made such outrageous claims.

It is with ironically hateful language that he tries to convince his followers that certain Americans hate this country. A month before this tweet, at the kickoff rally of his 2020 campaign in Orlando, Florida, he told the crowd, "The radical Democrats, driven by hatred... are out to destroy you, and they're out to destroy this country." This language is completely unacceptable.

(Democrats serve in uniform, including combat zones. Americans of all political beliefs put their lives on the line so that all citizens can join the party of their choice, vote for the person of their choice. His declarations were so improper that the Secretary of Defense and the Joint Chiefs were put into an unprecedented position—the Commander in Chief verbally attacking members of the military and their families. If the president had said that Jews, or blacks, or Hispanics were out to destroy this country the implication would have been clear—there is no difference.)

7/21/19 *"I don't believe the four Congresswomen are capable of loving our country..."*

The nickname, The Squad, was given to four female members of Congress, Alexandria Ocasio-Cortez of New York, Ilhan Omar of Minnesota, Ayanna Pressley of Massachusetts, and Rashida Tlaib of Michigan (all minorities, two Muslim). His bigotry is thinly disguised as he assigns himself godlike qualities judging that they are not "capable" of love. It is actually the narcissists who are incapable of love, or incapable of expressing what we consider a normal semblance of a loving relationship. It is the lack of sympathy and empathy that handicaps them. All those with personality disorders have problems with what mental health professionals call object relations (relationships with other humans), multiple affairs, multiple marriages, the number of people dismissed or fired, etc. can be an indication of this, but more important is the inability to adequately judge friend (of democracy) from foe, which has become a national security issue under this president: Vladimir Putin (Russia), Kim Jong-un (North Korea), Mohammed bin Salman (Saudi Arabia), Recep Erdoğan (Turkey), Rodrigo Duterte (Phillipines), Viktor Orbán (Hungary) are favored and praised while our allies (and these Congresswomen) are denounced and betrayed.

8/16/19 *Rep. Tlaib wrote a letter to Israeli officials desperately wanting to visit her grandmother. Permission was quickly granted, whereupon Tlaib obnoxiously turned the approval down, a complete setup. The only real winner here is Tlaib's grandmother. She doesn't have to see her now!*

He uses a request from a member of Congress to visit an elderly family member to make some political hay. This is unprecedented for sure, below the dignity of the office of the president, without question, but let's examine the words used because they reveal so much. The president uses the word obnoxiously as if his judgment is everyone's. His judgment is final. He goes so far below the belt as to tell us that the real winner is the sick grandmother who doesn't get to see her granddaughter. The narcissist cannot feel sympathy or empathy and it is proven here. This is bullying behavior, the perverse pleasure gained by attacking someone when they are down. It is not a nationally important issue, like an enemy attack on our country, but it is all the same issue—the same brain, the same personality, must make decisions through the same filter; and that filter, unfortunately is always, "How does this affect me." Every situation for the narcissist must be twisted for maximum personal gain.

7/26/19 *The WTO IS BROKEN... NO more! ... I directed the U.S. Trade Representative to take action so that countries stop CHEATING the system at the expense of the USA!*

The World Trade Organization (WTO) deals with the global rules of trade between nations. The president has also said that NATO is obsolete. It's dangerous to have a dysfunctional president who sees every American alliance and partnership through the lens of a personal business transaction. Of course, like our military presence in South Korea, our relationship with NATO or the WTO have always been seen as an investment in liberty and justice, rather than as a financial burden we cannot afford. Secretary of Defense James Mattis resigned because of a strategic decision to withdraw from Syria but, as mentioned earlier, his resignation letter showed his larger concern for the degrading of the world order established since WWII. The narcissist makes sweeping generalizations (NATO obsolete, the World Trade Organization broken) about organizations that include many allies. No previous president made such declarations about complicated international networks involving friendly members, because no previous president believed that their personal judgment was greater than the collective wisdom of free nations.

8/7/19 *Just left Dayton, Ohio, where I met with victims and families, Law Enforcement, Medical Staff and First Responders. It was a warm and wonderful visit. Tremendous enthusiasm and even love. Then I saw failed Presidential Candidate (0%) Sherrod Brown and Mayor Whaley totally...*

The tweet starts out perfect, any president would mention meeting victims and families and praise first responders and medical personnel—completely normal. Then the tweet mentions tremendous enthusiasm and even love. Enthusiasm at a mass shooting? Enthusiasm for what? Love? Love is something that a narcissist has a hard time perceiving and expressing, and he proves that with his sign-off. He ends this tweet about a tragic shooting in Dayton by telling his millions of Twitter followers that he met "failed" Democratic Senator Sherrod Brown and lets us all know Brown's 0% poll numbers (as reported by the president). This is abnormal to an extreme. If you, a normal person, meet victims and families of victims you are affected; it puts you in a somber, serious, compassionate mood. Out of your sympathy, your empathy for the tragic loss of life, the heroic efforts of medical staff, you could never go on the attack of an opposition party politician—especially not the same day, not in the same announcement. But because we know the writer to be a narcissist, the first part of the tweet can be interpreted as, "look how wonderful I am going to the scene of the carnage" and the second part of the tweet is a disclosure of where the president's priorities really lie. He just met with the victims and grieving family members but none of their grief resonated. He takes the time to type the word "failing" in front of Sherrod's name and to tell us the percentage of voter support he received was 0%. This is a striking example of this pathology.

8/28/19 *I don't want to win for myself, I only want to win for the people. The News@FoxNews is letting millions of GREAT people down! We have to start looking for a new News Outlet. Fox isn't working for us anymore!*

This tweet is a confession of a very un-American idea. No American news organization should be working for the president. It goes against all the norms set up since the Constitution was written for a president to talk in this way. And in a fit of narcissistic wounding reminiscent of a jilted lover's rage, he urges millions of people to start looking for another news outlet because Fox, which has been the most loyal to him, frequently at the expense of accurate fact checking, aired something that he saw as critical. No previous president in my lifetime has been so ego-fragile as this—it meets the clinical criteria for character disorder.

(Character disorder, considered more pejorative, was renamed personality disorder but for the narcissist and individuals with antisocial leanings, the original designation is more accurate).

9/7/19 *Unbeknownst to almost everyone, the major Taliban leaders, and, separately, the President of Afghanistan, were going to secretly meet with me at Camp David on Sunday...*

This tweet is indicative of a person so thin-skinned that he must tell us what we didn't need to know in order to make himself look better. The buck never stops on his desk. "Unbeknownst to almost everyone..." simply means standard procedure for classified information: known to everyone who had a need to know, but not known to anyone who did not have a need to know. No previous president would have felt the need to tell us about a secret meeting that fell through. Good leaders do not talk about near misses.

It is dangerous that this president feels compelled to boast about things best kept secret due to their highly sensitive nature. We saw this when he revealed classified material about ISIS to Russian adversaries (White House, May 10, 2017) so sensitive that the details had been withheld from allies; but the Top Secret nature of this information was subordinate, in his mind, to his need to brag. We witnessed a similar display in the Oval Office when he bragged to enemy state diplomats (Russian) that he had fired the director of our Federal Bureau of Investigation.

Many in the news media and general public grasp how inappropriate his carelessness is. However, it is notable to the mental health community that the media does do not grasp how his language and actions fit a specific clinical diagnosis. The fear, the warning of so many clinicians is that without this understanding the country cannot realize how much danger is possible.

9/5/19 *The fake media was fixated on the fact that I properly said at the beginnings of Hurricane Dorian, that in addition to Florida and other states, Alabama may also be grazed or hit. They went Crazy, hoping against hope that I made a mistake (which I didn't) Check out maps...*

Under normal circumstances, this should never have been a news story. The president mentioned Alabama as possibly being in the hurricane's path (ultimately it was not). This never had to be addressed again, let alone maps altered with sharpie pens and government employees feeling pressured to defend the president's slightly mistaken forecast. These lengths the president went to defend his statement are noteworthy. Most adults understand that we all make mistakes. The president's response is that of a child defending himself against criticism.

He is so thin-skinned that he feels he must tweet a clarification to a previous email once criticized. What is so diagnostic is capitalizing the word 'crazy,' taking presidential time to tell the country in writing that others are hoping against hope that he made a mistake, and feeling the need to put in parenthesis that he did not.

This would all be insignificant if the same brain wasn't in charge of nuclear weapons and national security. This same tendency to alter facts, to pretend perfection, is pathological and inevitably has dire consequences on a larger scale.

This same psyche, incapable of admitting a simple mistake about a weather forecast, had to defend himself against allegations of accepting help from a foreign adversary to win an election and being caught on a recorded telephone call making a quid pro quo ("which I didn't")—so we get the same distortion of the truth—"the call was perfect." We witnessed the same denial of truth when the president was confronted about false information he delivered concerning the pandemic (e.g., "Everyone who wants a test can have a test."). This is what the military does not allow, especially of a leader. You cannot blatantly lie to your subordinates with no repercussions. In a combat zone the results can be devastating.

Narcissists will try to persist until they wear out the audience—they want either their false claims to be agreed to, or the subject to be dropped. In the field of domestic violence the same pattern recurs, with the perpetrator gaslighting the victim.

9/16/19 *I call for the Resignation of everybody at the New York Times involved in the Kavanaugh SMEAR story...*

With this tweet the president, once again, shows his contempt for freedom of speech by attacking journalists covering the (now Supreme Court Justice) Brett Kavanaugh confirmation hearing—thereby violating his oath of office. But more revealing is his knee-jerk thought process, which not only reveals an emotionally volatile reaction to a news story, it also reveals a tendency to make proclamations, like royalty, he wishes he had the power to execute. He calls for the resignation of people as if this is one of the powers of the presidency.

He once tweeted (August 23, 2019, in response to Chinese tariffs), "Our great American companies are hereby ordered to immediately start looking for an alternative to China." Ordered! During the Covid-19 crisis he said that the powers of the president are absolute over the states. These types of comments become fodder for satire on comedy shows but they are not gaffes, and they are not funny; they are windows into his thinking.

9/23/19 *She seems like a very happy young girl looking forward to a bright and wonderful future. So nice to see.*

This tweet about Greta Thunberg, the young environmental activist, was pure sarcasm. It followed her making a speech to Congress (September 19, 2019) about global warming and about the threats, such as science denial, to continued environmental degradation.

Here is an excerpt from that speech:

> My name is Greta Thunberg, I am 16 years old and I'm from Sweden. I am grateful for being with you here in the USA. A nation that, to many people, is the country of dreams.
>
> I also have a dream: that government, political parties and corporations grasp the urgency of the climate and ecological crisis and come together despite their differences—as you would in an emergency—and take the measures required to safeguard the conditions for a dignified life for everybody on earth.
>
> I have a dream that the people in power, as well as the media, start treating this crisis like the existential emergency it is. So that I could go home...

12/13/19 *So ridiculous. Greta must work on her Anger Management problem, then go to a good old fashioned movie with a friend! Chill Greta, Chill!*

This is the leader of the free world... bullying a 16 year old. He must insult her, demean her, make fun of her. It should go without saying that this is bizarre, improper behavior. Many days I feel the public would need none of my training and experience to get that this is an abnormal mind. This is an ego so fragile that each wounding (however slight) creates a compulsion to respond, to defend. This has very dangerous implications.

Why is this tweet so revealing of narcissistic character structure? The presidency of the United States is the most important job in the world. It requires daily attention to matters of national and international security. No president should have the time to respond to perceived criticism from one teenager. But the narcissist never forgets an insult (Rosie O'Donnell) or a compliment (Vladimir Putin)—this president cannot resist attack or counter-attack, even toward a single individual if they ruffle his feathers. It bears no resemblance to good mental health.

10/16/19 *What is happening to President Trump with impeachment is a Constitutional Travesty.*

The only oath that the president takes is to defend the Constitution. In this tweet, not only is he not protecting it, he is spreading a falsehood (to millions), that a legitimate, legal process is a travesty. He knows (or should know) that impeachment was instituted by our Founding Fathers in the Constitution. Yet, the narcissist will choose personal survival over the survival of others, even over the survival of democracy. Here lies the heart of the threat to the nation; the lack of awareness among the vast majority of citizens of the danger of this character structure, the very real threat of having a president who not only cannot "defend the Constitution against all enemies," but shows admiration for our dictatorial enemies over our allies who share our democratic values. This has never before happened in our history.

11/7/19 *...The Lamestream Media, which is The Enemy of the People, is working overtime with made up stories in order to drive dissension and distrust!*

This tweet is more than just clinical; it's a disqualifier from federal service. The president starts with sophomoric name-calling but then devolves into anti-American rhetoric, calling the media the enemy of the people, which is again, a violation of his oath of office. Only a pathological narcissist would engage in this blatant projection in order to accentuate "dissension and distrust" in the country. The president has had many briefings concerning Russian efforts to use our media to do just that, spread dissension and distrust. The narcissist's behavior is aiding and abetting an enemy's strategic objective. When former President George W. Bush made a rare public speech in response to the "enemy of the people" quote he reminded us that the press was not always kind to him but that it was essential to a free society. That was normality. That was leadership.

11/7/19 *...Nowadays they don't use "Fact Checkers" anymore, they just write down whatever they want."*

The narcissist's agenda is to discredit anything said against them. With previous presidents there was an allegiance to the checks and balances on power, including free speech, as an essential part of preserving our "grand experiment" of democracy. A narcissistic president is incapable of seeing the virtue of the limits on presidential power. This explains bizarre statements such as "maybe I could pardon myself" (if the Mueller investigation led to conviction in the Senate) or "maybe the people won't want me to leave office." The narcissist feels entitled to unfiltered speech—it is up to us to set the limits.

His comment about shooting someone on Fifth Avenue and not losing one voter was a precursor to scores of inappropriate comments by a Commander in Chief. Unfortunately, and a narcissist doesn't get any luckier than this, people keep rationalizing each inappropriate utterance as being due to his uniqueness as a politician without realizing that his "uniqueness" is not unique to the mental health profession. Whether it is an incident with one individual, such as sexual assault, or whether it is harm to a larger group such as immigrant children, Kurdish fighters, or Syrian refugees, the compassionate part of the brain, the compassionate part of the psyche is undeveloped.

11/12/19 *The circus is coming to town. The corrupt, compromised, coward and congenital liar Adam Schiff Show on Capitol Hill, brought to you by his raging psychotic Democrats and the top allies in the Media Mob. Everything you're going to see in the next two weeks is rigged...*

In this tweet he calls the Chairman of the House Intelligence Committee, Representative Adam Schiff, corrupt (no record of corruption) even though he is the one who lost a federal lawsuit (his university) and a New York lawsuit (his charity) due to his own corrupt practices. He also calls Adam Schiff a congenital liar, a very interesting choice of words, and incredible irony, since it is the president who has told the highest number of lies in recorded presidential history.

He calls Democrats psychotic, which not only insults Democrats as he intended, but also demeans the office of the presidency by using slanderous language. He throws the media into the mix calling it "a mob" so that he can continue an oft-repeated false, yet to him necessary, claim that legitimate media is fake (anything negative toward narcissists is wrong in their mind).

The narcissist, like a shark that cannot stop moving or it will die, does not see nor care about hypocrisy. They will frequently use words and phrases like "honestly," "trust me," "believe me," "to tell the truth," even as they are lying to you.

11/12/19 *...This is a phony showtrial. There is zero due process, none, it is yet another witch hunt. This is what the Socialist Democrat Party has become. There's not one thing the Democrats have done in the past 3 years except try...*

This tweet illustrates the president's classic pattern of reporting his own version of reality, hoping it wins out in the end. It is a form of brainwashing, classic propaganda strategy. First he calls the House impeachment hearings a show trial, knowing the Senate conducts the trial portion of the impeachment process. He uses a constitutional safeguard "due process" inaccurately; his intent is to degrade the constitutional process despite the fact that he is the only fraud involved, as proven by legitimate legal proceedings.

He also uses the term witch hunt to pound the theme of the innocent being falsely tried and judged. One of the most dangerous aspects of this president has been his promoting conspiracy theories and giving credence to groups whose doctrines are based on conspiracy theories. This includes alt-right and white supremacists groups as well as Vladimir Putin, who has pushed the "Deep State" conspiracy and made it a major theme of his Radio Sputnik broadcasts within the United States. This conspiracy theory that there is a deep state within the U.S. government plotting to overthrow the sitting president is an insult to all dedicated public servants, particularly in the intelligence community, and especially in the FBI, which the president claims without proof, has "corruption at the highest levels."

It is the duty (particularly due to Putin's involvement) on the part of our elected representatives to set the record straight to the American voting public.

On November 28, 2017, the president re-tweeted an alt-right, anti-Muslim video from England to millions of Twitter followers.

To use the highest office for such endorsements far exceeds impropriety, it falls into the realm of clinically diagnostic and shows character abnormality. He had already legitimized the alt-right in America by his grotesque response to the Charlottesville riot ("fine people on both sides"), now he was doing it in Britain and internationally—completely unprecedented—only a narcissistic or antisocial character could degrade the office of the president for such an outrageous violation of democratic principles. Yet, individuals with a personality disorder fail to understand what is wrong with their inappropriate behavior and language.

This president has already stated that the Geneva Conventions tie our hands, that he would not want to jeopardize business deals over the murder of a journalist, he told us that he fell in love with a mass murderer. These are completely deviant declarations at odds with international law and our nation's military doctrine, the military he now commands. He sets the example for all those below him. It is painfully transparent why he degraded three American war heroes, praised and pardoned a war criminal. What is frustrating for mental health professionals is that none of this is surprising. The only thing surprising and utterly unacceptable is that he continues to command.

11/12/19 *...to hurt Donald Trump and we, the people who support him. The left has never accepted the results of the 2016 Election. They never saw this coming. This is not just about President Trump. They hate everyone he is representing."*

This tweet is one of the most important of his presidency because it reveals why he is unfit to be President of the United States. It is a shame that his hate speech has progressed to the point where many of his victims are shocked into stunned silence.

This tweet has two extremely important elements. The first is a major strategy of his to keep repeating that any opposition by Democrats (in Congress or the voting public) is the result of them not being able to accept the results of the 2016 election. He has repeated this so often that when Republican members of Congress cast their vote against the articles of impeachment many of them repeated this assertion.

The second part of this tweet is what makes him unfit for command. He tells millions of Americans that his opposition hates everyone he is representing. The President of the United States represents every American. His job is to preserve the title "United States." Instead, this president divides, he stokes the emotion of hate for his own personal gain. He tells half the country that the other half hates them. Let's illustrate how obviously inappropriate this is with a different example: If a general told one group of soldiers that another entire group of soldiers hated them we would snuff that immediately. That's exactly what the president (the Commander in Chief!) did with this tweet. Again, people need to be reminded that there are Democrats in uniform serving in every branch of the military, stateside and in combat zones. This statement not only insults them and the sacrifices they are making for their country, it potentially alienates them from their brothers and sisters in arms. The Joint Chiefs could have commented on these two divisive tweets about a party that many people in uniform belong to.

This is the dangerous war of attrition of this presidency. This is the kind of dysfunction familiar to military clinicians experienced with individuals with personality disorders—their beliefs disqualify them. This is why our country is in trouble. We have a leader in charge of organizations that would have to dismiss him if he was an employee—a double standard, blatant hypocrisy, a house divided that cannot stand.

12/20/19 *I guess the magazine, "Christianity Today," is looking for Elizabeth Warren, Bernie Sanders, or those of the socialist/communist bent, to guard their religion. How about Sleepy Joe? The fact is,*

no President has ever done what I have done for Evangelicals,
or religion itself!

This tweet is further evidence of the extreme level of narcissism dominating this president's thought processes. The first part of the tweet continues the theme that his opponents have a socialist/communist bent, thus contrasting MAGA to socialism/communism: introduced as his campaign theme at his Social Media Summit, July 12, 2019. The second half of the tweet is bizarre, almost delusional, (although it does not meet the criteria of psychosis, he does not suffer from psychotic symptoms such as delusions and hallucinations). His condition is much more dangerous than that (psychotic patients do not survive in politics or the military, their symptoms too severe, too debilitating to hide). The statement "no President has ever done what I have done for...religion itself!' resembles magical thinking combined with a thinly veiled reminder to Evangelicals that he is their religious standard bearer. In a clinical setting we would be asking the patient to explain how he believed he has done more for religion itself (with an exclamation point). The answer to that question would be quite revealing of the patient's overall character structure and his/her fitness for duty, especially leadership. Remember, this is a man who said in his inaugural address that his campaign was "A historic movement the likes of which the world has never seen." We have never heard such grandiosity from any previous president (and for good reason).

12/20/19 *It's time to put House Democrats on trial.*

Sometimes his shortest tweets reveal volumes. There is the simple attack on Democrats and his long standing strategy of reversal (like the FBI, the CIA, the DOJ needing to be investigated, not him) but more importantly this tweet again reveals that the President of the United States feels no obligation to preserve the checks and balances the founding fathers established. The narcissistic president, out of self-preservation, is attacking and trying to destroy our very system of governing. This is why comparisons to President Nixon are wrong—Nixon did not exhibit the criteria for a mental health disorder, and he was capable, for the good of the country, of being persuaded to resign. Narcissists only care about their own "good."

01/14/20 *The corrupted Dems trying their best to come to the Ayatollah's rescue.*

On Monday, January 13, 2020, the president re-tweeted a fake image of House Speaker Pelosi and Senate Minority Leader Schumer in Middle Eastern garb standing in front of an Iranian flag.

The photoshopped image showed Pelosi wearing a hijab and Schumer wearing a turban. "Democrats 2020" was shown below the pictures in text.

Again, there is an adolescent quality to his impulses, like a teenage bully's pranks; and if he were not the leader of the free world it might not be so disturbing. But it is so far below the dignity of the office of the presidency. His bigotry is on full display yet, like most racists, he is oblivious to the revealed prejudice against people who come from a culture where this is their daily dress; the photo is meant to be pejorative.

There is no behavior too base for the narcissist, there is only winning.

This explains why, as a candidate, on national television he called on Russia to spy on an American citizen (Hillary Clinton during the 2016 campaign). Unfortunately the narcissist's behavior can be so far outside the box that people do not know how to respond properly. The public's outrage on this occasion, as on many other occasions, was muted.

What was distinct, and what I loved about the military and military medicine is that we know how to respond to someone acting outside of the boundaries of our rules and regulations. We put the behavior to the test and soon discover that it is either correctable through discipline, or it is not correctable due to a pathological character structure—the latter we discharge for the good of the service.

1/20/20 *It was exactly three years ago today, January 20, 2017, that I was sworn into office. So appropriate that today is also MLK jr DAY. African-American Unemployment is the LOWEST in the history of our Country, by far. Also best Poverty, Youth, and Employment numbers, ever. Great!*

I would hope that anyone could see the abnormality of this tweet. On this national holiday it is traditional and expected that the president say something about the contributions to our history by the great civil rights leader Martin Luther King Jr. However the entire tweet is about himself; MLK Day usurped for a message about what HE has done for African Americans. His entire message turned into a vehicle for bragging. The level of narcissism is so abnormal that it should have been a wake-up-call for congressional leaders. The key clinical criterion, as indeed with so many of his tweets, is that the person tweeting is clueless to its inappropriateness (or he wouldn't have posted it). This reveals the thought process of the narcissist, an obsessive concentration on self—reminiscent of a tweet on Memorial

Day in 2017 where he said that our military heroes buried in Arlington would be proud of HIS economy. I marveled how that comment did not wake up more than two Senators from Arizona, one who spent more than five years as a POW (John McCain).

As I mentioned earlier, narcissists are anemic in the area of sympathy and empathy. They cannot connect emotionally to the sacrifice of others, so we are forced to suffer, on MLK Day, the president's omission of the sacrifices of Dr. Martin Luther King Jr., everything drowned in a flood of self-praise. Just as he took the sacrifice of John McCain and reduced it to ridicule ("I like people who weren't captured"). No president has ever before lacked sympathy and empathy to the extent that he could not emotionally connect to our national heroes.

The frustration of clinicians has been having to witness these deviant thoughts and words and beliefs go unchallenged, and even worse, watch millions of Americans hero-worship someone mentally unfit for office.

1/26/20 *Shifty Adam Schiff is a CORRUPT POLITICIAN, and probably a very sick man. He has not paid the price, yet, for what he has done for our country!*

This tweet has four separate elements, all of them indicative of this illness:

First, he capitalizes the word CORRUPT—it is one of his favorites. Unfortunately, the audacity of the narcissist frequently confuses those around him, those who are normal. Adam Schiff has absolutely no connection to corruption other than being an accomplished prosecutor. The president, on the other hand, has paid $27 million in fines for corrupt practices just since his election. The hypocrisy and projection of his accusations should be laughable, should be worse than laughable, a window into his complete unfitness for leadership. Those who back him have chosen to turn their gaze away from this inconvenient truth in order to continue their support.

Second, the president says that Adam Schiff is probably a very sick man. No previous president has used language like this about a political opponent; it is obscene for someone occupying our White House to make personal verbal attacks such as this. Every previous president had proper decorum but also the awareness that your political opponents have loved ones who would be hurt by below-the-belt personal attacks. It's just not done! Spouses and children are forced to endure public scrutiny when slurs come from the President of the United States. John McCain's daughter, Meghan, showed us her pain at her father's funeral, referring to the president's outrageous remarks about her dad and contrasting their shallowness with her father's unconditional sacrifice for this country. What has been unprecedented is the silence on the part of GOP leaders, who have failed to defend the president's victims, Republican or Democrat.

Third, the president delivers a threat—"he has not yet paid the price"—something also unprecedented for the White House. This is extremely dangerous. When the future 45th president suggested that some "Second Amendment" person might be able to stop Hillary Clinton from appointing Supreme Court Justices, the nation heard from Ronald Reagan's daughter, Patti. She was appalled at the remarks, having almost lost her father to a deranged shooter. She condemned the comments heard not only by many "sane and decent people" but also by someone "locked in his own dark fantasies." She concluded: "... words matter. But then you know that, which makes this all even more horrifying."

We had the *Baltimore Sun* shooting after "The press is the enemy" message. We had the Tree of Life Synagogue shooting by a self-proclaimed white nationalist a few days after the president declared himself a nationalist. We had the El Paso shooter fearful of Mexican immigrants. This followed many, many anti-immigrant, anti-Mexican tweets and rally speeches. We had a domestic terrorist mail bombs to individuals and to the news network CNN. Every one of those targets had suffered repeated verbal attacks by the president.

Only a narcissist or antisocial character could fail this responsibility. Jeff Zucker, the head of CNN, warned the White House that "words matter," after the mail bomb delivery to their headquarters. Any normal leader would cease calling CNN "fake news" at that moment, realizing that their words could be seen as a directive. With the narcissist that is not going to happen; they lack any normal level of empathy to relate to the victims of the crime.

Fourth, the narcissist does not see anything wrong with what they do. This is why you never get an apology. They do not hear anything inappropriate in their own words because these are their true beliefs. Others can try to sway them or educate them on what should be done, but they do not get it. This is why we saw the vacillation in Charlottesville, three separate messages on the same subject within three days as he monitored public reaction (the one thing important—the one thing that matters because it is survival). This is the President of the United States—knowledge about WWII and the Holocaust should have been enough to denounce Neo-Nazis, but to refer to them as fine people shows something much more pathological. White supremacy and racial superiority are forbidden within the United States military;

it is un-American, un-constitutional. For a military member the oath of office is a promise to defend the Constitution against all enemies, even unto death. For the Commander in Chief to be ignorant of this, for him to verbalize the virtue of domestic enemies, adds to the mounting evidence of those who see him as mentally unfit for command.

2/8/20 @RepDebDingell, who called me, tears flowing, to thank me for rolling out the maximum "Red Carpet" for the funeral of her husband, then voted against me on the partisan Impeachment Hoax, said "everybody (Dems) wants to get out of town. This has been my whole career, one of...

When you interview individuals with personality disorders, their abnormal responses to incidents, especially emotional incidents, are both striking and symptomatic. What's remarkable about this tweet about Representative Dingell, and so indicative of the narcissistic personality disorder (NPD) diagnosis, is both the lack of concern for the widow and the ability to attack her at her most vulnerable moment. The narcissist cannot relate to, i.e., feel that vulnerability. This, combined with his ever-constant self-congratulations, is practically a textbook case of pathological narcissism. He has the need to tell us that he rolled out the red carpet but the most important and disturbing part of the tweet is the "tears flowing." This mockery of her is completely pathological. It is not the act of any decent person, and it certainly has never been done by the occupier of the White House. For mental health professionals this is not foreign. This is the language typical of individuals with character problems. Their emotional reactions to human interactions are impaired, and they therefore struggle with relationships of all kinds.

This reaction (this tweet) resembles that of the president's tit for tat with Myeshia Johnson, the pregnant widow of Sergeant LaDavid Johnson (who was killed in Niger, West Africa, October 4, 2017). Under such circumstances, it should make no difference if the person is from an opposing political party or even if they dislike you. Speaking to a recent widow normally evokes an amount of compassion, sensitivity to their feelings during a difficult time. With character pathology that is impossible, so that a tragic situation (a widow with fatherless children) and the family's grief was multiplied by the insensitivity of the president.

2/18/20 These were Mueller prosecutors, and the whole Mueller investigation was illegally set up based on a phony and now fully discredited Fake Dossier, lying and forging documents to the FISA Court, and many other things. Everything having to do with this fraudulent investigation is...

This tweet is typical for this president, he exaggerates what little truth he can find and turns it into a falsehood. Inspector General (IG) Horowitz did find significant systemic problems within the FISA program (errors and omissions, even an email from another intelligence agency altered by an FBI lawyer), but he found no political bias and also found information that should have been in the FISA application that was not (errors of omission). The kinds of errors found by the IG were the type found in thousands of applications. The IG found no failures between the Justice Department and the court but rather within the executive branch. And the Steele Dossier has never been discredited. It is false that it was a fraudulent investigation. Moreover, the president calling the Mueller probe illegal is so outrageously false that it should have led to unanimous condemnation in Congress. It is a lie about investigating an enemy attack on our country. Every lawmaker in Congress knows there was nothing illegal about the Department of Justice inquiry. In fact, their own investigations, both Senate and House, confirmed the findings. All three investigations—DOJ, House, and Senate—reached the same conclusions: that Russia interfered with the 2016 election, acting against Hillary Clinton.

The only acceptable/expected response to enemy espionage against the U.S. would be for the president to acknowledge what was confirmed by our intelligence agencies and to reassure the American people that all measures were being taken to end it and to ensure that it never happened again. Instead the country underwent three years of the president's denial of facts. The three years of the president calling enemy espionage a hoax, the three years of his calling efforts to uncover Putin's cyber warfare "a witch hunt," are diagnostic evidence of NPD. Only an extreme form of narcissism would put self-interest over national interest. Only extreme narcissism lets narcissistic wounding (the idea that he needed enemy help to defeat Clinton) turn into betrayal of country, aiding and abetting a malign power.

6

RUSSIA, IF YOU'RE LISTENING

Mueller Testimony—July 2019

THE FORMER FBI DIRECTOR, Robert Mueller, confirmed that Russia engaged in an intensive campaign to meddle in the 2016 election and that those efforts would intensify in 2020 and that Congress must act aggressively. He said that this Russian effort was amongst the most serious challenges to democracy that he had ever seen in his career and that it deserves the attention of every American. Russian spies found the Achilles heel of the U.S.—dependence on public opinion and technology including social media, radio and television.

The candidate's presidential campaign had many contacts with Russian operatives and citizens—Paul Manafort's clandestine sharing of polling data with a Russian political consultant, Konstantin Kilimnik, and Donald Trump Jr. meeting Russian operatives in Trump Tower (June 2016)—these repeated findings did not rise to the legal definition of conspiracy. However, the Mueller probe found numerous incidents of interference by the president that did not exonerate him from obstruction (but the Justice Department Office of Legal Counsel had already rendered the opinion in 1973 and 2000, that a sitting president cannot be indicted; it did confirm that the president could be charged after leaving office).

Mueller said of the president's praise of WikiLeaks, which leaked emails stolen by Russia from Democratic entities, "problematic would be an understatement" because it encouraged illegal activity. During the two years of the investigation the president never agreed to meet with Mueller, yet he met with Russian President Vladimir Putin in person six times, called him 10 times and exchanged letters four times. A month before Robert Mueller's testimony to Congress about Russian cyber warfare against the United States, the president met Vladimir Putin at the G20 Summit in Osaka, Japan. When reporters asked whether Russian interference in our presidential election was a topic of discussion the president openly joked with Putin, playfully wagging a "scolding" finger—a bizarre, unprecedented reaction and a clinical red flag.

The Facts

A foreign government was trying to rig an American election. Yet, despite the fact that the then president-elect was briefed on the proof of Russian hacking, he went on national television during a widely viewed debate and warped reality—saying the source of the hacking could be China or a 400-pound person sitting in bed, thus discrediting American intelligence personnel.

Russia has been propping up right-wing groups in Europe who are xenophobic, nationalistic, anti-Muslim, and anti-immigrant, that want to weaken the European Union. These are all things the president does. It leaves us asking whether he unwittingly acts like an agent of the Russian Federation, or whether he has played a conscious part in weakening our allies.

Weakening the North Atlantic Treaty Organization (NATO) is one of Russia's premier policy objectives—the president has called NATO obsolete.

He told George Stephanopoulos, ABC News journalist, that Putin was not going to go into Ukraine and had to be told by Stephanopoulos that Putin was already there. He said that he had heard that the people of Crimea would rather be with Russia, regurgitating Vladimir Putin's talking points.

The electoral campaign of the president-to-be was interested in lifting the sanctions imposed on Russia for its invasion of Crimea and Eastern Ukraine and, in fact, National Security Advisor, Michael Flynn, was convicted on charges related to this.

During the Republican National Convention, campaign operatives worked on weakening the American stance on Russian intervention in Ukraine. The campaign manager, Paul Manafort received millions of dollars from pro-Russian entities in Ukraine, and campaign foreign policy advisors (Page and Manafort) met with senior Russian operatives, including Russian intelligence officers.

The president's financial ties to Russia are still under investigation. The candidate/president refused to release his tax records but he sold a mansion in Florida to a Russian oligarch for 54 million dollars more than he paid for it four years earlier. Speculation about money-laundering persists mostly because the president has been caught in numerous lies on the subject. The Mueller investigation revealed that the president continued to pursue the building of the Moscow Trump Tower while repeatedly telling the American people that he had no business deals with Russia.

(Pathological lying is a disqualifier and a diagnostic feature that is unacceptable in the military, and frequently the first identifier in the military of NPD).

Donald Trump Jr., quoted in the *New York Times*, said at a 2008 New York real estate conference, "Russia makes up a pretty disproportionate cross-section of a lot of our assets... We see a lot of money pouring in from Russia."

Felix Sater, the Russian-born former business associate of the president with ties to organized crime, a twice-convicted felon, proved to be an invaluable source to the FBI, which was able to use his ties to organized crime families in New York. Sater was pushing for a deal to build a Trump Tower project in Russia, he once escorted the president's children around Moscow, and was a business partner on the Trump Soho project in New York.

The Mueller investigation revealed that Felix Sater and Michael Cohen tried to back-channel a deal to the president that would have his administration drop sanctions on Russia imposed by the Obama administration in exchange for the Kremlin withdrawing troops from Eastern Ukraine and leasing Crimea for 50 to 100 years. The proposal came at around the same time that the National Security Advisor, Michael Flynn, was caught lying to the FBI concerning conversations with the Russian ambassador about removing economic sanctions on Russia.

The Results

Although the Mueller Report could not confirm criminal wrongdoing on the part of the president, it revealed someone unfit for office (someone doing numerous things to obstruct a criminal investigation of an enemy state). DOJ rules prevented the indictment of a sitting president or charges would have been filed. This is why he could not be exonerated. To those professionally trained to recognize personality disorders this was an inevitable conclusion. Narcissism prevents anyone from successfully assuming the role of public servant (e.g., military service). Instead, we have an individual committed to the art of the personal deal, many deals illegal (housing, charity, university), many deals circumventing public scrutiny and disclosure (his personal lawyer in Ukraine pursuing a quid pro quo with the Ukrainian president outside of the parameters of the State Department). In this sense the mere refusal to disclose tax records, that all presidents since Richard Nixon were open to, becomes a metaphor for his entire life and certainly the modus operandi for his administration.

His son-in-law, a White House advisor, tried to set up a secret back channel of communication with the Kremlin that would be invisible to the American people. The president eliminated the visitor log to the White House so the public could no longer know who visited "our house." He insists that his one-on-one meetings with Vladimir Putin be secretive, no longer public record, an act that says to the American people that we don't have a right to know what he is up to. There is always the same pattern; he pursues his personal agenda over our nation's agenda.

With his views about NATO, Brexit, the European Union and Syria, we have a president whose policy objectives align more with Vladimir Putin and Russia than they do with the United States. The resignation of Secretary of Defense James Mattis highlighted this and his words should have been a wake-up call for the country, or, at the very least, for Congress.

I do not hear enough public resistance to these unprecedented actions. There is a disturbing lack of recognition on the part of the voting public that there is a specific mental health issue that would explain all these anti-American actions. We, the American people, continue to ignore the obvious—there has never been an American president who would ever have contemplated any one of these things (there has never been a president portraying this psychiatric profile).

7

THE PRESIDENT UNPLUGGED

ON FEBRUARY 16, 2017, THE NEW PRESIDENT addressed the nation during a White House news conference, covering a wide range of topics. He named his new labor secretary, spoke about the resignation of Michael Flynn, relations with Russia, immigration, the media, the confirmation process, the economy, foreign affairs, the build-up of the military, etc. It was an early indication of what we could expect from a leader untethered to the truth. He trashed previous administrations with distortion after distortion, but the goal of his message (echoing his inauguration speech in which he referred to "American carnage") was to paint the picture that he inherited a mess. Although Russian contact with his campaign and interference in our election were vital topics of distortion, his remarks about his Electoral College victory, much like his obsession with crowd size, were an early example of a clinical problem. He received 306 electoral votes but he described this victory by saying, "I guess it was the biggest Electoral College win since Ronald Reagan." False. Barack Obama won 332 electoral votes in 2012 and 365 in 2008. Bill Clinton secured 379 electoral votes in 1996 and 370 in 1992. Why is this important? The president knew that this claim could be easily contradicted by fact checking but he did not care. We were witnessing something completely new in American politics: a president willing to create an alternate reality, one he fully expected the public to swallow. For clinicians this was all too familiar, and unsettling to see it in the White House.

This was an unprecedented danger for our country. In this same press conference, when speaking about the Affordable Care Act he said, "Obamacare is a disaster... they fill up our alleys with people that you wonder how they get there, but they are not Republican people that our representatives are representing." Our representatives? This quote, bizarre in its phrasing, ushered in the trend of splitting the country by party, and favoring one over another. No previous president abandoned the role of leader of all Americans. Our national motto: E PLURIBUS UNUM (out of many one) was replaced within one month of his inauguration with a decided favoritism for one group of Americans over another. It was about to get much worse.

The president loves to say the direct opposite of the truth: "The most transparent presidency in history," is one of his favorite phrases. In reality he has shut out the American people from White House operations and created a new level of secrecy. As previously noted, he eliminated the White House visitor log and his son-in-law, Jared Kushner, tried to set up a private communications channel between the White House and the Kremlin outside our intelligence communities. Kushner himself could not even pass his background investigation; he was denied a security clearance, which the president overrode. Before long the White House press briefings were eliminated and the president has kept the content and record of his interactions with Vladimir Putin totally secret. He has had the phone records of conversations with Putin and the Saudi royal family put in a highly classified server (as we learned from the whistleblower when phone records of talks with President Zelensky, of Ukraine, were placed in the same server).

The president creates phrases that have no connection to reality, "Mueller and his 17 angry Democrats." He repeats them over and over and over until they become the mantra of his followers. "Russian hoax," "witch hunt," "fake news," all absurd but normalized for some through repetition. Congressional leaders certainly know what's false; by allowing his lies to go unopposed his enablers become part of the lie. We do not allow lying to go unchallenged in any other organization but suddenly it was permissible for the President of the United States. After an interview on national television (June 16, 2019) where the president told ABC News reporter George Stephanopoulos that he might accept help from a foreign country in a future election, the Speaker of the House of Representatives, Nancy Pelosi, said that the president can't tell right from wrong. Whether the Speaker knew it or not, this is literally true for the individual with NPD. Evidence was building, based on this very diagnostic feature that would lead to impeachment.

The future President of the United States said the following during the Commander in Chief Forum (September 8, 2016)– "Putin has great leadership over his country ... more than our president has been a leader."

This language is anathema for the leader of the free world. It demonstrates either profound ignorance of the atrocities committed by a dictatorship or worse, admiration for them. Secretary Mattis resigned partially because he saw this tendency: the admiration of dictators and trashing our allies. The president has kept none of it a secret because narcissists don't recognize that anything is wrong with their thinking. They experience all of their thoughts as normal. They also experience their actions as normal, they are puzzled and angry when they have to explain to others what they have done "wrong" because for them it is not wrong. Since it is the feeling portion of the psyche that is so impaired in the narcissist, they admire material accomplishments rather than morality.

He made the "perfect" call to the Ukrainian president although he requested an investigation of his new political opponent, Joe Biden, in the 2020 election cycle (proving what he's said—that he would again accept help in an election from a foreign nation). He simply cannot accept its illegality. He has praised Putin and the young Saudi Prince Mohammed bin Salman, even though they are both murderers. He fawned over Kim Jong-un and told us how smart he was, how impressive that a 27-year-old took over and ran a country. He said nonsensical things such as Kim's people support him, and Putin has an 82% approval rating in Russia.

He congratulates dictators on fraudulent election victories (again not something any American president has ever done) yet he has had nothing but criticism for NATO and our European allies. His operatives have favored Russian-backed entities in Ukraine. Short of his actually being a Russian agent, a suggestion which mental health professionals do not support, a clinical condition is the only thing that makes all of this anti-American/anti-ally activity make any sense.

In an interview with Bill O'Reilly, the conservative FOX TV host, the president shocked O'Reilly by his cavalier attitude toward Putin being a killer. He brushed it off by making a false equivalency with the United States ("what, you think our country's so innocent?"). He received criticism for these remarks, even from conservative circles. Most of those who disapproved merely heard it as unpatriotic. Mental health professionals heard something different, something familiar with a clinical explanation.

It is a national tragedy that the voices of my profession, the experts in personality assessment, speaking out from a duty to warn, have been almost entirely ignored. The president has a long history of declarations which represent a very consistent pattern of thought—from his minimizing the 1989 Tiananmen Square Massacre by the Chinese Government/Military in which thousands of student protestors were murdered ("they put it down with strength... America isn't strong anymore"), to the cavalier view of the mutilation and murder of journalist,

Jamal Khashoggi by Saudi Arabia ("the world is a dangerous place"), to the bromance with the sadistic Kim Jong-un ("we fell in love"). The shame is that the lack of knowledge concerning this particular mental disorder has resulted in American leadership doing nothing to prevent this narcissistic personality from undermining our democratic institutions. (The White House ignored all subpoenas issued during the impeachment hearings. The president denied a Covid-19 pandemic information/strategy update to the U.S. House of Representatives because they are "Trump Haters"—he then accused our elected representatives of the following: "... they frankly want our situation to be unsuccessful, which means death... they want us to fail so that they can win an election.") The American people need to understand more than this type of language being inappropriate or unprecedented for the President of the United States, they need to understand that it is indicative of a specific mental disorder which would render one unfit for command.

The lack of sympathy and empathy, indicative of pathological narcissism, was shown early in the president—a history of cheating contractors and workers at his resorts and clubs, real estate brokers who sold his properties, even law firms who worked for him. He has been involved with over 3,500 lawsuits. He filed for bankruptcy four times (Trump Taj Mahal, 1991, Trump Plaza Hotel, 1992, Trump Hotels and Casinos Resorts, 2004, and Trump Entertainment Resorts, 2009). Although lawsuits and bankruptcies have no connection to mental illness, per se, his business dealings/record, to include his rental properties, university and charity, fit a manipulative and exploitive profile of the narcissist and antisocial character. His mentor, Roy Cohn, legally representing crime bosses, was eventually disbarred. What is diagnostic of the narcissist and antisocial character is comfort with criminals and illegality due to the lack of a moral compass. This thread goes forward to dealings with Russian oligarchs, and illegal activities that ended with his personal lawyer, his campaign manager and national security advisor being convicted and sentenced to prison. His long-time personal friend and political consultant, Roger Stone, was also convicted of activities linked to Russia but the President of the United States publicly shows contempt for our legal system by attacking the verdict and considering a pardon. Again, illegal behavior is not necessarily connected to mental illness, but characterizing all the indictments and convictions of his associates as part of a giant conspiracy involving a "Deep State Justice Department" is extraordinarily abnormal and thus the greatest evidence of this diagnosis. Logic and reasoning alone dictate that the president, more than any other American, bears the responsibility of defending and preserving the integrity of the FBI, CIA, judiciary and legislative branches that embody the government he leads.

It makes no difference to the narcissist how many people are inconvenienced or suffer (children separated from their parents and put in cages, Kurdish civilians and fighters abandoned in the middle of war) as long as they accomplish some personal objective. The individual with narcissistic and antisocial traits cannot feel the pain of others; they don't care because they can't care. On a small scale this is why they can easily victimize family members, on a larger scale they can use the instruments of power for self-satisfaction.

His lack of sympathy and empathy was also displayed when, on December 22, 2018, the U.S. experienced a federal government shutdown as the president and Congress could not agree on an appropriations bill to fund the operations of the federal government for the 2019 fiscal year. The shutdown ran for 35 days and cost the American economy at least $11 billion. The president demanded that the appropriations bill include $5.7 billion for a U.S.-Mexico border wall. The Republican-controlled Senate unanimously passed an appropriations bill without wall funding. The president refused to support the bill—800,00 federal employees and one million federal contractors were out of work because he wanted to fulfill a personal campaign promise to build a wall on our southern border and Congress did not allocate the funding he had requested. This was a narcissistic act; again his personal wishes more important than hardship to almost two million dedicated workers. He then said that if he did not get the funding he requested he would declare a national emergency. On February 14, the House and Senate passed an appropriations bill funding the government until September 30, the end of the fiscal year 2019. The bill included $1.3 billion for fencing along the U.S. Mexican border. On February 15, 2019, the president declared a national emergency concerning the southern border of the United States. By declaring an emergency he was able to divert $3.6 billion assigned to military construction. This declaration was unprecedented in that none of the 58 previous emergency declarations by U.S. presidents involved circumventing Congress to spend money it had expressly refused to authorize or allocate. The president used terms like "invasion" of our southern border but Congress passed a joint resolution to terminate the national emergency. The president vetoed it but that congressional vote, by itself, proved that there was no national emergency, only the personal agenda of a narcissist trumping national interests.

The president, as a candidate, speaking in Michigan (August 12, 2015) saw someone in the audience hold up a copy of *The Art of the Deal* and he said "my second favorite book." He told the audience that it is one of the greatest books. But in a statement of "modesty" that is completely diagnostic he admitted that there was a book greater than his. "Nothing beats the Bible, not even *The Art of the Deal*." One of the diagnostic features of personality disorders, and this is especially prominent in sex offenders, is their lack of awareness when they have said something inappropriate. To even suggest in jest that your two favorite books are the Bible and your own is a shocking confession of narcissism but it is the ease with which it is done and the lack of embarrassment for the pairing which marks the language as clinical. The comfort with which the narcissist includes his book with one of the most famous inspirational texts in human history is a striking diagnostic feature lost on many because he makes so many outrageous claims so frequently.

In October 2018, bombs were mailed to the houses of Barack Obama, Hillary Clinton, George Soros, to CNN headquarters and others who had been verbally targeted by the president. When a 56-year-old man, Cesar Sayoc, was caught in Orlando, Florida, Sayoc's van had pro-Trump stickers plastered all over it. This was an important diagnostic moment—the president's failure to address this connection. Any previous president, seeing those images would have felt obligated to address the American people to clearly separate himself from anyone who might misconstrue a message and believe they were doing the president's bidding by attacking his political enemies. The problem with this, of course, is that it would be hypocritical because this president has used language so hateful ("lock her up,"/"Obama created ISIS,"/"the press is the enemy," etc.) that it is near impossible to disconnect him from culpability. The president's language could easily be understood as a call to action, particularly for the mentally unstable; but a narcissist cannot grasp the inappropriateness of their behavior so it continues unabated.

On August 3, 2018, a mass shooting occurred at a Walmart store in El Paso, Texas. A gunman shot and killed 23 people and injured 23 others. The Federal Bureau of Investigation investigated the shooting as an act of domestic terrorism and a possible hate crime. The shooting has been described as the deadliest attack on Latinos in modern American history.

After this mass shooting, former Texas Representative, Beto O'Rourke eloquently told the nation that words are important. He outlined how the shooter drove 600 miles to kill Mexicans and the shooter's confiscated computer later showed that the killer was obsessed with the Southern "invasion" of our border by "Hispanic" immigrants. The shooter's language mimicked that of the President of the United States. When the president arrived in El Paso, he met with victims and families, as expected, then went off on a tangent about his previous visit and the crowd size. He said, "We had twice the number outside. And then you had this crazy Beto. Beto had, like 400 people in a parking lot." It is amazing that these abnormal diatribes do not result in universal condemnation and recognition of impairment. A normal person who arrives at the scene of a mass murder is emotionally influenced by the tragedy, acts in a somber way that comes from being engulfed in incredible sorrow. Yet this president (to give us a picture that was worth more than a thousand words), instead requested to see the orphaned infant who lost both parents in the shooting, and posed with a big smile and a thumbs-up for the cameras. It was surreal, profoundly distressing and it was clinically informative.

Thirteen hours after the El Paso shooting, another occurred in a nightclub in Dayton, Ohio. The president traveled to meet with victims and first responders but then, following his usual blueprint during national tragedy or disaster, tweeted personal attacks of local politicians and compared their popularity to his own. This is proof of the lack of empathy for the victims he was there to comfort. But the narcissist cannot comfort, the sympathy and empathy needed for that are precisely the mental impairment. The only thing that matters to the narcissist is the narcissist, a major disqualification for fitness of command. In the military we realize that disaster is inevitable when working with a person with a personality disorder and why it's our duty to remove them for the good of the service.

8

BIGOTRY AS NORMALITY

NO MEMBER OF CONGRESS should have remained silent about the promotion of the Birther Movement that began in 2008 to discredit Barack Obama and deny him the presidency. It was the beginning of accepting absurdity by one political party in order to gain a possible electoral advantage; it was also the beginning of abdicating power to a racist conspiracy-theory candidate. Once you allow falsehood to replace truth, you are complicit—precisely as Senator Jeff Flake warned his colleagues. What he understood is that it had the potential to destroy the entire system, all of our democratic institutions. That promotion of false information not only revealed the character of the candidate, but also revealed deeply held beliefs, as already evidenced by other actions. Let's review:

The president's father was arrested in 1927 while participating in a KKK rally. This was his legacy, and father and son were sued in 1973 by the Nixon Administration for racial discrimination in their New York rental properties. They counter-sued but their suit was dismissed and they were forced to comply with the Fair Housing Act. In 1989, responding to the Central Park jogger rape case, where a white woman was brutally attacked and raped by unknown assailants, the future president took out full page ads in the New York newspapers. He called for the death penalty for the five adolescents of color who were falsely accused and imprisoned. They were later cleared by a confession to the crime and DNA evidence; but he doubled down again on their guilt, many years later, when the adolescents, now well into adulthood, were released.

On March 4, 2017, in a tweet, the president accused his predecessor of spying on him. It was typically unsubstantiated. He referred to President Obama as a "bad (or sick) guy." It was a continuation of his racism but it was more than that, it was an extreme example of pathological narcissism. It was a dramatic flouting of all previous norms.

No president had ever accused a predecessor of wrongdoing with zero evidence; but referring to a former president, especially one still living (and the president's wife and children still living) as a "sick guy" was unacceptable, unprecedented language for a president. And once again, the critical clinical component was the inability of the perpetrator to see anything wrong with his words, nor to care about their impact.

In February, 2017, during a White House Press briefing, the president asked a black reporter, April Ryan, if she could set up a meeting with the Congressional Black Caucus. The president asked her if they were "friends of hers." It is in those moments that he most reveals himself. His racism comes through the most when he is unguarded—a question from a reporter that he couldn't anticipate. To ask this black journalist if she could set up a meeting between the President of the United States and members of Congress is an absurd question for anyone except a racist and a narcissist. A key narcissistic component is that everyone in the room but him knew the inappropriateness of his suggestion. Racism is not synonymous with narcissism but narcissists remain at odds to social norms that represent moral and cultural awareness.

On October 1, 2018, in the Rose Garden of the White House, the president had this exchange with ABC News' Cecilia Vega:

President: "She's shocked that I picked her. She's in a state of shock."

Reporter: "I'm not, thank you Mr. President."

President: "That's ok, I know you're not thinking, you never do."

The president has such a comfort with bullying behavior, insulting and degrading people comes as easily as breathing to him. It is not presidential, to say the least, but this exchange reveals a great deal more. In this case it is no accident that he is addressing a female. He has a long track record of degrading females.

Twenty-five separate women have accused the president of sexual misconduct, but it is his response to the allegations that is so revealing of sexual deviancy. When confronted with specific allegations he has smugly said of an accuser: "she's not my type" as an argument to why it didn't happen. During one presidential debate, when confronted by Fox News host Megyn Kelly about his disparaging remarks about women ("fat pigs,"/"dogs,"/"disgusting animals") he responded, "only Rosie O'Donnell," proving on the spot her very point. But he didn't stop there, he then went on the attack of Kelly telling the press that she should apologize to him, that there was "blood coming out of her eyes, blood coming out of her, wherever." He has no decency filter, nothing is off-limits. In another presidential debate, this time with Secretary

Clinton, he told an audience of millions that she was a "nasty" woman. These thoughts are easily verbalized and he never apologizes. The problem is that his thoughts and actions do not represent public sentiment or cultural norms. The narcissist isn't merely out of touch with proper etiquette, they do not see the value in it.

The "Unite the Right "rally was a white supremacist and neo-Nazi rally conducted in Charlottesville, Virginia, August 11 to 12, 2017. It had been planned for months, since April 2017, when the Charlottesville City Council decided to remove the statue of Robert E. Lee. Promotional material, especially those approved by the neo-Nazi, Richard Spencer, listed well-known white supremacists and a holocaust denier. The organizers stated point of the event was: "If you want to defend the South and Western civilization from the Jew and his dark-skinned allies, be at Charlottesville on 12 August." It spoke volumes that the president initially refused to denounce David Duke, Richard Spencer and the White Supremacist movement, knowing that they admire him and hail him as their standard bearer.

(At an alt-right rally in Washington D.C., November 19, 2016, Richard Spencer exhorted the crowd, who responded with Nazi salutes, "Hail Trump, hail our people, hail victory." Spencer called for "peaceful ethnic cleansing" and resurrected the German word "Lüg-genpresse" referring to the mainstream media—a word used by the Nazis to attack critics.)

The death of Heather Heyer, a 32-year-old paralegal, struck and killed by a car deliberately driven into the counterprotestors by a white supremacist, should have made the president's remarks of condemnation easy and unambiguous. Instead, we got an argument for a false equivalency. It would be ignorant enough for "John Doe" to say there were fine people on both sides but for the President of the United States, who gets a daily intelligence briefing, and whose Justice Department has a domestic terrorist watch list, there is no such excuse. And as Commander in Chief there was no excuse for describing hate groups, whose members would be disqualified from military service due to unconstitutional beliefs, as "very fine people." This wasn't just ignorance, this was further confirmation of a narcissistic character structure overriding American Constitutional guarantees.

There are many examples of this president's inappropriate behavior and comments, especially toward minorities and women. These are easily accessible online: His *Playboy* interview, his *Lifestyles of the Rich and Famous* interview, his *Access Hollywood* interview, his *Howard Stern Show* interview, his characterization of minorities as rapists and murderers and terrorists, his contempt for immigrants coming from "shit-hole" countries (Haiti, El Salvador and African countries), telling four Congresswomen of color to go back to where they came from (three of the four born in the U.S.). Ignorance of critical history, and racism, are not proof of a clinical issue. Bigotry is not synonymous with mental illness; however, it is his operating as if it is normal for the President of the United States to promote bigotry that makes his actions diagnostic.

9

THE RALLIES

DURING HIS CAMPAIGN the candidate held 323 rallies (186 primary season and 137 general election). He has had 88 more since occupying the White House. Just the fact that the president continued campaign rallies after assuming the presidency is bizarre and a powerful message that rather than being laser-focused on the most demanding job in the world, much of his time and energy will be devoted to staying in power. It was also an instant message that he does not see himself as president of all Americans, the rallies being partisan to the extreme. Right from the start his rhetoric was about dividing the nation, name-calling his opposition with inappropriate personal attacks, as well as ethnic slurs and maligning religious minorities. His invocations did not mirror the religious diversity of our country, were not nondenominational, but rather showed a blatant preference for fundamentalist Christianity in a way that violated the separation of church and state, as well as the norms of presidential behavior.

While previous presidents have expressed personal faith in God, professed Christianity, and incorporated elements of their beliefs in certain national rituals, like prayer breakfasts, this White House has taken it to the extreme by selecting clergy to do invocations at rallies who have asked for God's blessing for victory over the opposition party. Pastor Ed Young, who was chosen to do the invocation for the president's Houston rally (October 2018), belted out, "Will we continue to be a Republic under God, or will we slouch toward Godless socialism?" The crowd cheered during his "prayer." He preaches that the Democratic Party is actually a Godless religion. For the president to willfully be associated with this kind of message is further proof of a diagnosis that impairs the acceptance of "One nation, under God, indivisible..."

Despite the fact that he is Commander in Chief, and his only oath is to defend the Constitution, that founding document of our democracy, against foreign and domestic enemies, this president displays no understanding of the building blocks of our government and individual rights protected by the Constitution. The first amendment guarantees that government will not sanction one faith over another.

> *Congress shall make no law respecting an establishment of religion, or prohibiting the free exercise thereof; or abridging the freedom of speech, or of the press; or the right of the people peaceably to assemble, and to petition the Government for a redress of grievances.*

Thus, the military has chaplains representing different faiths but there is no officially sanctioned government religion. No chaplain could ever call on God to favor a political party. Atheists, also, are welcome to join the military and enjoy the same rights of citizenship as the most devout worshipper. Every military member has sworn, even unto death, to protect individual freedom of belief and expression.

Yet this president violates the first amendment constantly. As reflected previously, freedom of speech and press are under constant assault and he has called any criticism of him or his policies "fake" and journalists "the enemy of the people." This language betrays our country; for it to be coming from the White House is unacceptable—it can only have dangerous consequences.

The president failed to separate himself from alt-right manifestos: as stated previously, he re-tweeted a series of alt-right, anti-Muslim videos posted by the leader of a far-right group called Britain First. These videos were inflammatory, showing violence by Muslim extremists. They were intended to incite fear of and anger toward immigrants. UK Prime Minister Theresa May put out a statement saying that the reposting was wrong. I refuse to believe that you have to be a mental health professional to see that this is unprecedented and deviant. It is unconscionable that it would be the act of an American president.

On January 9, 2020, at a rally in Toledo, Ohio, the president said about Democrats: "They are vicious, horrible people... they are horrible people... they have never been more extreme, they are stone cold crazy... what they do to people is a disgrace." These remarks themselves are a disgrace. They are divisive. They are a betrayal of his office and like so many of his declarations at his campaign rallies, should have brought condemnation within Congress and even the Pentagon because of the military personnel serving overseas in combat zones defending this and other countries who are members of that party. It is just unacceptable that these service men and women could be called vicious, crazy and a disgrace. We all have family members who are Democrats; no president has the right to slander them, and no president has ever done so before. The narcissist holds up a mirror of projection, his words apply to himself: "vicious, crazy, a disgrace" and totally unacceptable. It is not good enough that Congress and military leaders recognize this; it is so inappropriate that it must be opposed. The president continually victimizes individuals or groups with impunity. There is only one reason.

On November 1, 2019, at a rally in Tupelo, Mississippi, the president started the rally by calling himself "the best president we've ever had," but he was just warming up. He told the crowd "the media and the Democrats have been involved in a corrupt partnership to thwart American democracy by any means necessary." This language is so hateful, so much an abdication of truth, that it is dangerous. He said that Democrats are "mentally violent." Think about that message. Think of the implications. Think how sick, how abnormal it is for the President of the United States to stand before an audience of thousands and tell these citizens that other citizens, in another party, are mentally violent. There is only one motive possible for such hate speech, a motive unacceptable for an office that carries the obligation of national unity. It is the type of language that has led to atrocities in other countries.

On July 24, 2018, at the 2018 Veterans of Foreign Wars National Convention in Kansas City, Missouri, the president continued his habit of inventing "alternative facts." It is a disturbing thing to watch someone who has no allegiance to truth give an hour speech based on the premise that the audience is either too ignorant to recognize a series of lies, or that they do not care. The entire speech went from one inaccuracy to another. He continued the lie that he created the VA Veteran's Choice program, which in fact was instituted by the Obama administration. I personally had been enrolled in that program for a couple of years when I first heard him tell Matt Lauer, during the Commander-in-Chief Forum, that he was the author of this idea. He also told the Kansas City rally crowd that he created the first walk-in mental health services. In fact, the VA had this option for decades. They are called Vet Centers and any combat veteran can walk in to any Vet Center without an appointment. I know this because I ran a Vet Center for five years following my military retirement. The speech had lies from start to finish. It is untenable for the United States to have a leader who refuses to tell the truth and if a country agrees to that it abdicates all power to the leader. As we see in the Communist systems we have opposed since WWII, when the leader cannot be held accountable for his speech or actions, freedom no longer exists.

To give up that freedom voluntarily is to commit national suicide. What this president does is simply repeat the same phrases over and over in speech after speech (a Nazi propaganda technique), until they become implanted in the minds of the listener. A sampling of his descriptions of Democrats at this rally:

"They want open border and crime's okay."

"The Democrats want to abandon ICE."

"Low IQ Maxine Waters and Nancy Pelosi have launched vicious smears on people who protect our communities."

"They want to get rid of the crime fighters."

Of course all of these claims are nonsense but not to his audience, and that is the unacceptable situation we find ourselves in with a pathological narcissist as president—an incessant, continual effort to divide the country. When the president said farewell to the VFW crowd in Kansas City he went into a recitation, "One nation, under God," and stopped right there—a very accurate place for him to end because the next word is "indivisible" and the next phrase is, "with liberty and justice for all," which proclaims the highest goal and ultimate trust of this high office, one which he is incapable of honoring.

On June 18, 2019, at the official launch of his campaign for a second term in Orlando, Florida, the president took his anti-American rhetoric to a crescendo:

"Our radical Democrat opponents are driven by hatred, prejudice and rage. They want to destroy you and they want to destroy the country as we know it." One is practically rendered speechless by such a quote coming from the President of the United States. It simply betrays everything we stand for as a nation. No previous president has gone on record telling one group of Americans that another group of Americans hate them. No previous president has said that one political party was out to destroy this country. Every American should have seen this president for what he was at that moment. Certainly members of Congress and the Joint Chiefs of Staff should have realized that a line had been crossed. Generations of Americans in my lifetime, WWII veterans, Korean War Veterans, Vietnam Veterans and the War on Terror Veterans amongst them, have been members of both major political parties. That is their right, a right they fought for—I will repeat until I am out of breath the simple fact that we currently have Democrats, in uniform, in combat zones, defending this country. I have seen young Americans killed and maimed for the ideals of this nation. The fact that the Commander in Chief was saying that some people in uniform, serving this country, were full of hatred, prejudice and rage, and that he, who had never served, felt the right to say that military members belonging to that group were out to destroy this country, went to a level beyond obscenity to betrayal of country.

However, I am not writing as an Afghanistan veteran so much as a clinician. I do not want to write out of my anger but out of clinical experience. The president's anti-American belief system is best understood (I believe only understood) by recognizing it as being due to a high level of narcissism. A level of narcissism that, if diagnosed in any service personnel, would lead to their obligatory discharge from the United States military. There is no doubt that if anyone within the chain of command below the president had made exactly the same comments, his or her career would be over. No one is above the law and the Commander in Chief's beliefs are in violation of the UCMJ (Uniform Code of Military Justice).

The Youth Rally

The president attended one "rally" that was not for adults, the Boy Scout Jamboree in West Virginia, on July 24, 2017. He addressed a crowd of thousands of adolescent boys and gave the most offensive speech I have ever heard given to the youth of America. I am an Eagle Scout so I am well aware of the values and principles that scouting is designed to instill. It is an organization committed to producing ethical, moral, upstanding American citizens and human beings. The president used the occasion to deliver a political stump speech and it was much more than inappropriate, it was clinical evidence of a diagnosis. He spoke to these boys who came from families representing the diversity of America and told them, "...under the Trump Administration, you'll be saying 'Merry Christmas' again when you go shopping." The Boy Scouts of America is non-denominational and non-political. He bragged about his red state victories over blue states. He was derogatory toward our previous president. He told these young men that Washington, the seat of our government, was a swamp, a cesspool, and a sewer. We teach these youngsters to revere our institutions of government. Invoking the Scout Law to accentuate loyalty, meaning personal loyalty, he had the audacity to use the word trustworthy (he who has been mandated to pay millions in fines to his victims). In a statement that some would think was delusional, but actually reveals a pathological level of narcissism, he said, "... an unbelievable tribute to you and all the other people that came out and voted for Make America Great Again." These were young teenagers (not only do they not vote but many would have parents who voted for his opponent). I don't believe I have ever witnessed a more striking example of someone self-obsessed.

10

THE BUCK STOPS
EVERYWHERE ELSE

WHEN BULLIES ARE NOT STOPPED they will continue the inappropriate behavior; when the bully is the most powerful man in the world the consequences are devastating. What we have witnessed over the three years of this presidency are personal, nasty and totally fallacious attacks on members of Congress, the FBI, the CIA, the DOJ, an entire impeachment process and the dedicated public servants who testified there, as well as many of the congressional members questioning them. He asked members of the Supreme Court to recuse themselves on any cases that might involve him or his family. When he pulled out of Syria, he lied about military operations in a combat zone and betrayed an ally on the battlefield. He is currently lying about medical facts and American lack of preparedness for a pandemic. The nation cannot afford a leader who unscrupulously, defensively and randomly invents "alternative facts" on the fly. We are now in the middle of the worst health crisis in a hundred years with the anticipation of one to two million Americans being infected with the coronavirus and a predicted 147,000 deaths by August, 2020. And as on every other subject during this presidency we cannot rely on the truth from our leader, to the contrary.

Some of his quotes about Covid-19:

"But it's something that we have tremendous control over."

"A lot of people think that goes away in April with the heat."

"Within a couple days it is going to go down close to zero."

"It's going to disappear. One day—it's like a miracle—it will disappear."

"Now the Democrats are politicizing the coronavirus... And this is their new hoax."

"I felt it was a pandemic long before it was called a pandemic."

"Anyone who wants a test can get a test."

"We're very close to a vaccine."

"I like this stuff. I really get it... every one of these doctors said,

'How do you know so much about this?' Maybe I should have done that instead of running for president."

"No, I don't take responsibility at all."

"I don't need to have the numbers double because of one ship that wasn't our fault."

"Our people want to return to work. They will practice Social Distancing and all else, and Seniors will be watched over protectively and lovingly. We can do two things together. THE CURE CANNOT BE WORSE (by far) THAN THE PROBLEM!"

"I'm not a doctor. But I'm like a person that has a good you know what."

As on any subject, the president has a team of experts advising him but the narcissist always knows better than everyone else. What is so dangerous is that he consistently follows all the same patterns: misinformation, bullying journalists and attacking news agencies who are trying to inform the public about the truth, downplaying anything that can make him or his approval rating look bad. In essence, everything that requires sympathy, empathy, and truth (the exact areas of dysfunction in the narcissist) is distorted and manipulated.

Recent clinically relevant events:

On April 3, 2020, he announced that certain states were not "vulnerable" to the virus—completely negating any scientific understanding of the disease, and completely contradicting his own national experts. Why would a president behave so irresponsibly? The only answer lies in the mental impairment that allows the individual with NPD to push their personal understanding/agenda as superior to everything else.

On April 12, 2020 the president re-tweeted a call to fire Dr. Anthony Fauci (one of the world's leading experts on infectious disease and part of the Covid-19 task force). The tweet ended with "Time to#-FireFauci." Our world is in the throes of a deadly pandemic. Dr. Fauci is an international expert who served six administrations (Democrat and Republican). When asked why he re-tweeted the message the president said, "I re-tweeted somebody, it doesn't matter." Was that a coward's way out? Yes! Did it show a total absence of leadership? Of course! But what is pathological is that it is a lie! The President of the United States posted that tweet deliberately and for a very clear purpose. This form of narcissism wants it both ways: discredit and disparage Dr. Fauci (#FireFauci) and at the same time keep him as an expert at task force briefings. This is called gaslighting and it creates mental confusion.

On April 15, 2020, the president verbally attacked the World Health Organization (WHO), deflecting any personal blame for a slow response to the pandemic. The gist of his complaint was the WHO believed false information that China was feeding them. Consistent with this level of narcissism, criticism of the actual liar, China, was absent from his comments. The other thing indicative of this disorder is the inability to see the illogic of the argument—praising President Xi for his transparency and thanking him on behalf of the American people (the tweet, 5:18 PM, January 24, 2020), but continuing to vilify the WHO and withdrawing funding. The narcissist needs someone else to blame. In this case it is the weaker WHO versus the powerful economic giant, China. No thought is given to all of the good the WHO does in developing countries with malaria, malnutrition, maternal and infant mortality, EBOLA, etc., but rather a personal spat between the president and the organization, which must be punished. It is not normal and we would have never seen this scenario with any previous president.

Also, on April 15, 2020, the president said the following, "When somebody is the President of the United States, the authority is total. And that's the way it's got to be. It's total." Does anyone need further evidence of the unconstitutional thinking of this president?

There is a serious gaslighting (brainwashing) technique that is being foisted on the American public by this president during these task-force briefings. It is the phrase "fake news." It is how a perpetrator gets a victim to abandon logic and reasoning. No President of the United States listens to fake news, for the simple reason that it is fake. Nor does any president listen to fake intelligence or a fake weather report. The very fact that certain news agencies are invited to the White House proves their legitimacy. The very fact that the president reads and listens, and frequently quotes these individuals and agencies, further confirms that they are credible. What is his motive for calling legitimate news organizations and reputable journalists fake? Ultimately, an extreme narcissistic character attempts to discredit everything but one voice. Of course, that would be anti-American, that would be a dictatorship.

During this crisis we are witnessing strong diagnostic indicators, epitomized in the president's ongoing interaction with our nation's governors. When the president perceived criticism he announced that governors needed to be more appreciative. He told his vice president, "Don't call the woman in Michigan." He meant Governor Gretchen Whitmer, who was experiencing a spike of cases in her state. He referred to Governor Jay Inslee of Washington, as a "failed presidential candidate" with 0% vote and a "nasty person" and a "Snake." To be able to do this at all, let alone in the middle of a crisis is sick, a sign of an incredibly fragile ego. It is a pathological mind that resorts to bullying during an emergency. The pleasure he gets from demeaning others in crisis shows the sadistic/antisocial qualities. He tweeted that his coronavirus TV ratings rivaled the finale of *The Bachelor*. This goes beyond abnormal to the ludicrous/surreal (Americans are dying and he is announcing his media popularity). It's no small thing; it is diagnostic evidence.

He also took time from the Coronavirus Task Force briefing to tell us about a drug interdiction mission and he held a Rose Garden press conference introducing the CEO of MyPillow, who gave us an evangelical view of how "a nation had turned its back on God" until the 2016 election. There is almost a carnival-like atmosphere to some of these broadcasts that the president controls, which, during any normal presidency, would be aimed at presenting the most trustworthy, scientific, data-driven information to an anxious public. Instead they are grist for the mill of late-night comedy shows, and above all, they are all signs of the president's abnormal mental status.

From George Washington to Barack Obama, all presidents needed to consult experts. They don't know more than their generals or scientists. Only a narcissist operating on a pathological level trusts their "gut more than other people's brains," but that is the inconvenient truth we face. The Pandemic Preparedness Office, which was part of the National Security Office, was dissolved by the president in 2018, and even this easily verifiable fact is turned into a lie, a specific lie described as the unpreparedness of his predecessors (he has been in office over three years). He, like all narcissists, is incapable of taking responsibility for anything.

All previous presidents have understood, no matter the outcome, that the full responsibility rests with them, or as President Truman famously put it: "The buck stops here." For the narcissist the buck stops everywhere else. The president actually said that, on camera! What is diagnostic, again, is the lack of awareness that there is anything wrong with that statement. He has done this throughout his presidency—recites anti-American beliefs, what would be disqualifying beliefs for any military member, and yet has no idea that anything is wrong with what he is saying. We have never seen this level of pathology at this level of government.

11

A CLEAR AND PRESENT DANGER

ON THE 25TH OF MAY, 2020, an African American man, George Floyd, was apprehended for passing a twenty-dollar bill suspected of being a forgery. He was subdued, handcuffed and put to the ground. A bystander filmed the arrest and police brutality on their cellphone while bystanders pleaded for the victim. The video went viral. The world was able to watch George Floyd suffocated by a cop who kept his knee to his neck until he was lifeless. The nation exploded. There were protests against this modern-day lynching in every major city in the country and in front of American embassies overseas. The overwhelming majority of protestors were peaceful; some of the protestors engaged in looting, vandalism and arson.

For a solid week there was mostly silence from the White House as tens of thousands of Americans took to the streets to make a national statement that black lives matter. The president was able to articulate cursory condolences from the Oval Office and at Cape Canaveral where he went for the space launch, but no speech devoted to the incredible national response, no comfort, no guidance, no consolation to a country in turmoil. His Twitter account was active with bullying one person or another. He had plenty to say about governors and mayors who could not keep law and order. He was obsessed with the looters but no interest or awareness about the pain and suffering of the African American community or what possibly made this go nuclear. He demanded National Guard involvement and deployed active duty military to quell the civil disobedience. He mocked political leaders of cities that did not have strict control. He called himself the law and order president. He sat bunkered, with his bunker mentality, and simmered for six days.

On Monday, June 1st, he had a conference call with the nation's governors and belittled anyone who did not have strict control over "the battle space." American citizens had taken to the streets from the

Atlantic to the Pacific and he failed to address the reason why the country was grieving and angry.

He said the protesters needed to be dominated. He started the day with a call to Vladimir Putin and as if echoing Soviet history he told the governors, "I wish we had an occupying force." He added, "Other countries are watching us and saying what a pushover." His language was almost identical to his infamous *Playboy* interview where he praised the Chinese government for the way they put down the Tiananmen Square pro-democracy protestors with "strength" (it was a massacre). He said, "Study Occupy Wall Street, it was an hour of bedlam but how it ended was a beautiful thing."

He expressed great emotion with the governors about a video he'd seen from Dallas where a white man, wielding a machete, was beaten by a bunch of protestors. The president was livid, "I've never seen anything like it in my life." He said over and over, "it was a disgrace." For a solid week most of the rest of America had repeatedly watched an unarmed black man in Minnesota slowly and deliberately strangled to death by a racist cop, but our Commander in Chief could say with a straight face, and the emotion of outrage, that he'd never seen anything like the non-lethal violence inflicted on someone in Dallas with white skin. The president, like most narcissists and antisocial personality disorders, and this is especially prevalent with sex offenders, had no idea that he had made a confession. Like the declaration that you can grab women by the genitals if you're a star or his joyful announcement that he fell in love with one of the worst human rights monsters on the planet, the person demonstrating character pathology is oblivious to the immorality of their personality structure.

Later that day, the president decided that he would walk to St. John's Episcopal Church one block from the White House and pose with the Bible in his hand for a photo op—no speech, no scriptural reading, no attending religious services, no message of comfort or hope, just a symbolic confession of the depth of his connection to holy scripture. The problem with this was that peaceful protesters had to be cleared from Lafayette Square for him to make that trek. Federal forces were dispatched (using rubber bullets, tear gas and flash-bang grenades) against people exercising their first amendment rights, in order to clear the space for a publicity stunt. Luckily for this nation, that was too much for many. Former presidents, religious leaders and retired flag officers went public with their condemnation of this show of force. Former military leaders specifically rebuked the Secretary of Defense and the Chairman of the Joint Chiefs of Staff for their participation in this abuse of executive power, the violation of the constitutional rights of their fellow citizens.

Secretary Mattis did a great patriotic duty with his condemnation of this violation of the constitutional right of our citizens to protest peacefully. He denounced the abuse of executive authority and the way this president divides us, pits citizen against citizen. Secretary Mattis clearly articulated the danger this leader presents even without a clinical awareness of any specific pathology. The ability to absorb and revere the virtues of our constitutional guarantees, or even the basic belief that all are created equal, are severely challenging to the narcissistic and antisocial character structure. The present danger is even greater because the charisma of this particular person has the ability to coerce others to abandon the principles they have sworn to defend. Fifty-two members of the Senate voted for acquittal on one article of impeachment, and 53 on the other, although there was overwhelming evidence of guilt. He had succeeded in bullying elected members of Congress to betray patriots who selflessly testified as whistleblowers against wrongdoing. He succeeded in coercing members of an entire party to ignore overwhelming evidence of obstruction of justice concerning an enemy attack on the United States. The president's lawyer, Michael Cohen, had warned others about following in his footsteps. He said that when you go to work for this man you find yourself doing things you never imagined.

On Friday, June 5th, Donald Trump was falsely accused of saying that George Floyd was looking down from heaven and would be happy at the upturn of our economy (as the president had once tweeted on Memorial Day when speaking of our military dead). During the president's economic speech, he had a brief aside on racial equality. He said that George Floyd would be happy to see what was happening in this country. The implication was that the massive display of solidarity, the nationwide protests declaring that black lives matter, would lead to social change. Of course it was presumptuous to suggest how an African American murder victim might feel, it was, to say the least, poor timing and must have been jarring for the Floyd family to hear. It was also disingenuous! By the end of the day the president re-tweeted a video of a black Trump supporter telling the conservative TV personality, Glenn Beck, that George Floyd was "not a good person." The narcissist has no moral compass about any issue, really, so the personality disorder traits spill out unfiltered. He negated all of his politically correct public statements of remorse over the killing of George Floyd in one tweet. At a moment when the only news story for two weeks was the massive uprisings in every major city in America over injustice, the President of the United States spread a derogatory story about George Floyd to millions of his Twitter followers.

Bigotry is not synonymous with a personality disorder so a bigot can stay closeted if they so choose, and not risk public disclosure of their true beliefs; but a bigot with personality disorder gives himself away. Their true feelings slip out and they don't have a clue why it's inappropriate. The president had taken criticism for not addressing the national outrage and grief over a blatant murder caught on video. He lashed back saying that the fake news media was trying to vilify him. He referred to his speech at NASA on May 30th and said that he honored George Floyd before he spoke about the space program. Like many things this president says there can be a shred of truth within the bigger lie he is trying to sell. The president did start his speech saying what happened in Minneapolis was a tragedy and that he had reached out to the Floyd family. He devoted 30 seconds to that family and the national trauma. He then spent the next 10 minutes talking about the need for law and order—a catch phrase for many meaning an excuse for police brutality. He praised the police who "protect us from gangs and drugs." He slipped into campaign-rally rhetoric saying that the looting and violence were caused by "radical left terrorists." This was unacceptably transparent. Anyone familiar with his rallies knows that one of his oft-repeated catch phrases is "radical left Democrats." A narcissist believes in their own cleverness, their own ability to deceive but they also don't care about anyone's feelings but their own. This is why each unacceptable utterance is never revisited, let alone worthy of an apology. At a time when our nation was torn asunder and needing comfort, guidance and healing, our leader was saying in code that Democrats (left wing) were terrorists and responsible for the nationwide violence. It was the exact divisiveness that General Mattis felt obligated to verbalize after the president mobilized active duty troops to put down a legal demonstration by U.S. citizens. His rhetoric promotes hatred, the kind that invites vigilante justice, the kind we had recently witnessed with the hunting down and killing of Ahmaud Arbery while he was out jogging.

What makes his vilification of half of the country (Secretary Clinton won the popular vote by 3 million) so much more unacceptable is that it is the exact strategic objective of Vladimir Putin, as disclosed in all three federal investigations into Russian cyber warfare. Rather than asking his 50 governors what they had discovered about the protests in their own states, Trump told the governors that Antifa and the radical left were the ones fomenting the violence and destruction. He offered not one shred of proof. He told them, "This is like Occupy Wall Street. It was a disaster until somebody said, that's enough and they just went in and wiped it out and that's the last time we ever heard the name Occupy Wall Street." Another confession! Like his admiration of the Chinese Communist government's handling of the Tiananmen Square uprising, the president is turned off by any show of dissent and turned on by crushing it. He joked with President Duterte in the Phillipines about the press being spies and he remained friendly and admiring of the young Saudi prince, despite proof that Salman had the journalist, Jamal Khashoggi, killed and dismembered. His particular pathology is so pronounced that he has said publicly how popular Putin and Kim Jong-un are with their own people. He says it with a straight face. These are his true beliefs. If there is no dissent then the leader is loved. With this president human rights violations are no impediment to friendship. If he stays in power we will lose our raison d'etre.

On April 14, 2020, the president tweeted:

> Tell the Democrat Governors that 'Mutiny On The Bounty' was one of my all time favorite movies. A good old fashioned mutiny every now and then is an exciting and invigorating thing to watch, especially when the mutineers need so much from the Captain. Too easy!

Like so many of the president's messages this one is a bit bizarre and calling for a mutiny seems counterintuitive. But he inadvertently provides a slip-of-the-tongue remedy. Apparently he missed the point of the movie: that the crew, pushed to the limits by a sadistic commander, Captain Bligh, must rise up against him and set him adrift.

12

CONCLUSION

Where Do We Go From Here?

MANY PEOPLE SAY THE ONLY WAY to correct this debacle is with the national vote in November, 2020. I certainly hope that every eligible citizen exercises their constitutional right to vote and that each (perhaps influenced by unfolding evidence) does so with a deeper understanding of what's at stake for our democracy if the current president remains in the White House. However, the nation will remain in constant potential danger if it takes that long to resolve.

The House of Representatives could initiate impeachment proceedings again for obstruction of justice on the part of the president in the investigation of Russian interference in an American election. The evidence is too overwhelming to be ignored and the number of indictments and convictions that came out as a result of it are too significant for an enemy attack to be labeled a hoax. But this process also takes time, and time is running out. We need action from leadership that will halt the steady erosion of our democracy.

The 25th Amendment could be invoked. The odds against it may be steep. It is unprecedented that a president be removed because he "is unable to discharge the powers and duties of his office" due to mental unfitness. With the whistleblower disclosures and other testimony concerning Ukraine we seemed to be following the scenario usually seen in the military: mental unfitness leads to violation of law, violations lead to discovery, discovery leads to discharge (or jail); or, in this case, unfitness leads to violation of law, violations lead to impeachment, impeachment is the mechanism for removal from office. But that was not the result and it would now require bravery and a breaking of "allegiances" of those required to invoke the 25th Amendment (the Vice President and Cabinet), choosing country over party. One may assume that those individuals, hand-picked by the president, might be hampered by a sense of loyalty or gratitude. It's also possible they see nothing disturbing or clinical in the president's behaviors. However, the latter is highly unlikely. It is practically impossible to work with a narcissist and not realize that something is seriously wrong. Anyone raised with religious principles, morals, ethics, a sense of decency, duty, honor and patriotism, must necessarily be stretched beyond their comfort zone working for this man. If they are true to their oath of office there will come a day of reckoning, an obligation to do their duty to protect the Constitution and the country no matter how uncomfortable personally. I am sure that many of the individuals of this administration listed in the prologue, those who were either fired or resigned, would fit this description.

Time For a Moment of Truth

I once had a young intern reach out to me, upset and confused about her clinical supervisor. She relayed that during private one-on-one supervision with her advisor he said to her, "I'd like to undress you." Then he paused and said, "Now what would you do if a client said that to you?" She was confused, she did not know what to do because she had never encountered this type of behavior in an authority figure.

It was a far cry from clinical supervision. But, like many a victim of harassment and sexual assault, she froze. She was willing to entertain the legitimacy of improper speech—she was thrown off guard. She needed an outside, objective view. Thank goodness she made the phone call because the perpetrator would not have stopped otherwise.

We, as a nation, have been exposed to similar behavior, completely unprecedented by anyone in this high position in government—rude, crude, abusive, cruel behavior coming from the one who is supposed to be our greatest protector. It has caused much of the society to freeze, not knowing exactly what to do because there is no precedent. It is a molestation of the psyche of America.

We know that we would not accept this behavior in a high school teacher or a Scout leader or any mentor or other authority figure. They would be reprimanded and/or removed from the job. Until now we have been clear who we want representing our community, teaching our children, what we want them to mirror. If we return to the values normally expected of political leaders, with any luck we will never be here again.

As It Stands

I wish this book could be considered completed but alas that is not possible. I am socially isolated at the moment, like most of America. I have spent the past several weeks listening to White House briefings on Covid-19, which meant listening to the narcissist dominate each briefing with false information, and ego-fragile tirades that demean the office of the presidency and victimize people (journalists, governors, scientists) dedicating their lives to their respective professions. In the past week, I have witnessed a president who is clueless how to address racial disparity and rage over inequality, due to his racist beliefs and white supremacy sympathies. He is also displaying his admiration for strongman tactics that mirror the dictators he has shamelessly told us he admires. It is a frustrating time because the question of why he behaves as he does is still not addressed. Certain news networks clearly recognize misinformation and improper behavior and try to inform the American people on the best way to live through our public health emergency, and they are tuned into the human rights issue spawned by the killing of George Floyd; other networks help spread "alternative facts" (as a White House spokesperson once claimed at the beginning of this administration). The informational divide we are experiencing perfectly aligns with Russian strategic planning and execution (as uncovered by the Mueller Report and the Senate and House investigations) and is a national security issue (thus the duty to warn—the impetus for this book).

There were three federal investigations into Russian interference in the 2016 presidential election, one in the Senate, one in the House of Representatives and one by the Department of Justice (commonly referred to as the Mueller Report). All three reached identical conclusions about the scope and intent of the Russian cyber warfare. All three give strong and detailed evidence of the Russian assault. The President of the United States has referred to these findings as fake, a hoax, and efforts to understand the depth/scope of Russian espionage a witch hunt. One message is a lie and the other the truth. The motive to lie is still in question, but the psychological profile which allows the lie is the subject of this book. I conclude with summaries of the three reports into Russian warfare against the United States.

Senate: The Select Committee on Intelligence (United States Senate on Russian Active Measures Campaign and Interference in the 2016 U.S. Election), concluded that the Russian government's attack on the 2016 election was the product of a deliberate, sustained and sophisticated campaign to undermine American democracy. The 67-page document went into great detail as to the specific actions by Russian intelligence to deepen distrust in our political leaders, to widen the divisions within American society, to weaken America's democratic institutions, to undermine confidence in our elections. The findings mirrored those of the Department of Justice (Mueller) and the House of Representatives investigations on Russian interference.

Nevertheless, the leader of the Senate, Mitch McConnell, has allowed the findings to be called a hoax and a witch hunt without speaking out against those lies or acknowledging that his silence further promotes the Russian agenda of sowing distrust in the electorate, and widening the divisions the Russian assault was meant to widen.

The Senate Intelligence Committee found that African Americans were the group targeted most by Russian social media trolls. They looked to stoke racial tensions and tried to convince African Americans not to vote, or to vote for Green Party candidate Jill Stein.

House: I include a letter from the Speaker of the House, Paul Ryan. *(see page 76)* The Republican Speaker's letter highlights the long time hostility of Russia and their efforts to undermine our democracy. He emphasizes the importance of holding Russia accountable for their attacks, and he confirms that there is no doubt that Russia interfered in the 2016 presidential election. He outlines the bipartisan bill signed into law, August 2, 2017, by President Trump, which punishes our adversary with economic sanctions. And he guarantees protection of Robert Mueller's investigation until completion.

Since the sitting president has done everything in his power to discredit and obstruct the revelations of the Russian attack on the United States, we face the most critical national security risk of my adult life. It is up to all of us to correct this assault on our republic.

Summary of the Mueller Report

Twelve Russian Army intelligence officers, NETYKSHO, ANTONOV, BADIN, YERMAKOV, LUKASHEV, MORGACHEV, KOZACHEK, YERSHOV, MALYSHEV, OSADCHUK, POTEMKIN and KOVALEV were indicted for conspiracy to commit an offense against the United States. The conspiracy involved hacking U.S. computers of persons and entities charged with the administration of the 2016 elections.

Paul Manafort: (Donald Trump's campaign manager), crimes included conspiring against the United States by illegally laundering offshore accounts, tax evasion, failing to register as a lobbyist, submitting false information to the Department of Justice, bank fraud, witness tampering, and breaching his plea agreement. He used his campaign role to angle for money from his wealthy patrons in Ukraine and Russia. His service for Trump coincided with the ramp-up

PAUL RYAN
1st District, Wisconsin

WASHINGTON OFFICE
1233 Longworth House Office Building
Washington, DC 20515-4901
(202) 225-3031
Fax: (202) 225-3393

TOLL-FREE: 1-888-909-RYAN (7926)
INTERNET: paulryan.house.gov

Congress of the United States

House of Representatives

Washington, DC 20515-4901

CONSTITUENT HOTLINE: **1-888-909-RYAN (7926)**   paulryan.house.gov | RSS | YouTube | Twitter

H Steve Nolan
Major, Usaf, Ret. (career Military and Afghanistan Veteran)
46 Sterling Street
Newtown Pa 18940, WI 53140

Dear Steve,

Thank you for contacting me with your thoughts regarding President Trump's meeting with Russian President Vladimir Putin in Helsinki, Finland, and the Russian government's efforts to interfere in and undermine the most recent United States Presidential election. I appreciate your taking the time to let me know your views on these important issues.

As I have long said: there is no moral equivalence between the United States and Russia. This is a menacing government that has time and again engaged in destructive, destabilizing activities that undermine democracy throughout the world. Consequently, I believe it is more important than ever for this Congress to focus on holding Russia accountable for its vile attacks on our basic values.

As you may know, the House has taken concrete action to counter Russian aggression. At the beginning of the 115th Congress, the House Committee on Intelligence initiated an investigation into Russian activities and intentions in the most recent presidential election. The scope of this undertaking included Russian cyber activity, counterintelligence concerns, and possible leaks of classified information related to the intelligence community's assessments of these matters.

On April 27, 2018, the House Committee on Intelligence released its final report on the bipartisan investigation into the Russian government's interference in the 2016 United States Presidential election. Should you be interested in reading the report, you may do so by visiting the House Permanent Select Committee on Intelligence's website here: https://intelligence.house.gov/news/documentsingle.aspx?DocumentID=882 .

Furthermore, the House passed H.R. 3364, Countering America's Adversaries Through Sanctions Act, on July 26, 2017. This overwhelmingly bipartisan bill, which was signed into law by President Trump on August 2, 2017, sent a powerful message to Russia: the United States will not tolerate provocative actions that stoke global instability. Should Congress find there to be additional sanctions that could be placed on Russia, I am more than willing to take them into consideration.

There is no question that Russia interfered in our election. While their interference had no material impact on the outcome of our election, it remains evident that Russia remains hostile to our most basic values and ideals. This is not just the finding of the American intelligence community, but also the House Committee on Intelligence. Should Vladimir Putin continue to undermine our interests, rest assured that this Congress is prepared to use every instrument of American power to defend the people we serve.

In your correspondence to me, you also shared your concerns regarding the Russian government's efforts to interfere in and undermine the most recent United States Presidential election. On May 17, 2017, the Department of Justice (DOJ) Deputy Attorney General, Rod J. Rosenstein, announced the appointment of Robert S. Mueller III – a former DOJ official and FBI Director under Presidents Bill Clinton and George W. Bush – to serve as Special Counsel to oversee and conduct the executive branch investigation into Russian cyber interference in the 2016 election. As I have said since the beginning, my priority has always been to ensure that thorough and independent investigations are allowed to follow the facts wherever they may lead, which is exactly what my colleagues on the House Intelligence Committee have been working tirelessly to achieve. I believe that Robert Mueller as special counsel is consistent with this goal, and as such, I value his role at the DOJ. Let me be clear, we will not interfere with this investigation, but instead allow it to take its course. Our country has a justice system that is based on the rule of law and no one is above the system.

Thank you again for contacting me about these important issues. Please know that I am aware of your views, and will keep them in mind as I work with my colleagues through the remainder of the 115th Congress. In the meantime, if you wish to share additional information with me concerning this issue, please feel free to contact me by calling, emailing, writing, or faxing me. Please be advised that mail sent to my office is subject to an additional delay due to increased mail security.

If I can be of further assistance to you, please do not hesitate to contact me. I am always happy to respond and be of service to you.

Sincerely,

Paul D. Ryan
Serving Wisconsin's 1st District

Letter from Speaker of the House Paul Ryan

of Russian intervention in the U.S. election and a ratcheting-up of Trump's pro-Russian campaign rhetoric.

Michael Cohen: Donald Trump's personal lawyer admitted arranging secret payments to women to keep them quiet about alleged affairs with Trump, and to lying about a Trump business project in Moscow pursued during Trump's campaign. He misled Congress. Those false statements were of national importance as they intentionally limited the ongoing investigations into Russian interference in a U.S. presidential election. He committed campaign finance crimes and lied to Congress and he committed the campaign finance crimes for the purpose of influencing the election. He stole millions of dollars from the IRS. Cohen was sentenced to three years behind bars, along with $2 million in penalties. In his final statements to the judge in the case, Cohen said that he had been living a personal and mental incarceration ever since he met the famous real estate mogul. He said that it was his own weakness and blind loyalty to Trump that led him to choose to participate in the elicit act of the president (campaign finance violations).

Roger Stone: a longtime Republican political operative and Trump friend, received a seven-count indictment alleging that Stone had tried to thwart congressional inquiries into Russian interference in the election. He was charged with lying to Congress, obstruction and witness tampering. The allegations suggest that the campaign was willing to seek out and use messages hacked by a foreign state (Russia) as political ammunition. The indictment detailed Stone's communication with Steve Bannon, who was then Trump's chief strategist and is identified in the indictment as a "high ranking Trump campaign official." Stone's testimony to the House Permanent Select Committee on Intelligence was deliberately false and misleading. He lied about documents pertinent to the investigation, about communication with his identified intermediary and his communication with the Trump campaign.

Richard Gates: (political consultant and lobbyist). In October 2017 Paul Manafort and Richard Gates were charged with various crimes in connection with work they performed for Russia-backed political entities in Ukraine. In February 2018 Manafort and Gates were charged with various crimes in connection with payments received for work performed for Russia for Russia-backed political entities in Ukraine. In February 2018 Gates pled guilty to multi-objects conspiracy and to making false statements. He plead guilty to conspiring against the United States, agreed that he evaded taxes, committed bank fraud and failed to register as a foreign lobbyist.

Michael Flynn: In December 2017 Flynn pleaded guilty to making false statements to the FBI about contacts with the Russian ambassador to the United States (links and coordination between the Russian government and individuals associated with the Trump campaign). Flynn submitted false information to the Department of Justice as he belatedly registered as a foreign lobbyist for work he conducted during the campaign to benefit the Turkish government.

George Papadopoulos, who served as a foreign policy advisor for the presidential campaign of Donald J. Trump, made material false statements and material omissions impeding the FBI's ongoing investigation into the existence of any links or coordination between individuals associated with the campaign and the Russian government's efforts to interfere with the 2016 presidential election.

Jeff Sessions had contacts with Russia's ambassador to the United States during the presidential campaign, contradicting what Sessions had told lawmakers during his confirmation hearing.

Mueller Report Conclusions

The Russian government interfered in the 2016 presidential election in sweeping and systematic fashion.

The Trump campaign had received indications from the Russian government that it could assist the campaign through the anonymous release of information damaging to Democratic presidential candidate Hillary Clinton.

The investigation identified numerous links between the Russian government and the Trump campaign.

(After the election the United States imposed sanctions on Russia for having interfered in the election).

Obstruction of Justice

The president asked his National Security Advisor, Michael Flynn, to resign when told about his lies to the FBI about his contact with the Russian Ambassador and their discussion of sanctions. The next night Trump asked the FBI director to a private dinner and said, "I hope you can see your way to letting this go, to letting Flynn go."

(What is diagnostic is the following: The president said he did not direct Flynn to discuss sanctions with Kislyak, but he said, "it certainly would have been okay with me if he did. I would have directed him because that's his job." The narcissist misses the lack of logic, or the inadvertent confession of wrongdoing. The president told the FBI director that Flynn was a "good guy." You don't fire someone who is a good guy and is doing what you would have ordered him to do anyway. No president should be describing someone who lied to the FBI under oath as a good guy but these things are invisible to the narcissist. Flynn was removed for the stated reason of lying to the Vice President, but as Commander in Chief he should have realized that lying to the second in command is in effect lying to the commander. The narcissist wants to split hairs that no one else would split. The president fired Flynn but said he was, "Just doing his job." It doesn't pass the test of normal thinking).

The president terminated FBI Director James Comey because Comey refused to publicly announce that the president was not personally under investigation.

The president told aides that special counsel had conflict of interest (unfounded).

The president immediately started tweets criticizing the Department of Justice and the Special Counsel investigation.

The president ordered the White House Counsel, Don McGahn, to have Mueller removed but McGahn threatened to resign rather than carry out the order. The president ordered McGahn to deny in writing that he had ever been asked to have Mueller removed. Again, McGahn refused this order.

The president asked K.T. McFarland, Deputy National Security Advisor, to write an internal email denying that the president had directed Flynn to discuss sanctions with Kislyak. She was not comfortable with this request and did not follow through.

The president's efforts to have Sessions limit the scope of the Special Counsel's investigation to future election interference was intended to prevent further investigative scrutiny of the president's and his campaign's conduct.

The president praised Michael Cohen when he falsely minimized the president's involvement in the Trump Tower Moscow project, then castigated him when he became a cooperating witness (Trump denied any business connections with Russia). Cohen also discussed pardons with the president's personal counsel.

The president engaged in public attacks on the investigation, non-public efforts to control it, and efforts in both public and private to encourage witnesses not to cooperate with the investigation.

The president-elect was briefed by intelligence personnel about Russian cyber warfare and its interference in the campaign. This included the fact that Russian interference was targeted to help his campaign and to damage Hillary Clinton. (He immediately went public casting doubt on our intelligence community and spent the next three years calling proven U.S. intelligence fake and a hoax, and efforts to uncover Russian espionage a witch hunt).

He denied that he knew of the Trump Tower meeting with Russian operatives to get dirt on Hillary Clinton (even though his son, son-in-law, and campaign manager attended) but in an interview with the *New York Times*, July 19, 2017, the president said that if someone called up and said, "By the way, we have information on your opponent... who wouldn't have taken a meeting like that." This was a display of unacceptable ignorance about the legal prohibitions on foreign interference in an American election. He repeated this when he told George Stephanopoulos, June, 2019, that he would accept such a meeting in the future if the opportunity arose. This is diagnostic of narcissists, their struggle with determining right from wrong. Normal people evaluate issues such as this by using their moral or ethical compass, but this does not happen with NPD. They put everything through the filter of their own personal benefit, exclusively—and they behave as if what they say is not shocking or controversial because to them it is not.

The letter from Attorney General Barr to U.S. Senate and House Judiciary Committees stated "while this report does not conclude that the president committed a crime, it also does not exonerate him."

By the next day the president was telling the American people that he was exonerated, in flagrant contradiction to the report on enemy interference. The nation, apparently so used to his lying, once again did not respond normally. This stop-the-presses moment was treated as if his almost daily lies on this subject were an alternative truth. This is not helped by the fact that congressional leaders, so partisan, fail to protect the American people from a foreign attack.

On May 6, 2019, more than 1,000 former federal prosecutors, who served under Republican and Democratic administrations, issued a joint statement maintaining that if Trump weren't President of the United States, he would have been indicted on multiple charges of obstruction of justice. The leadership in the House of Representatives decided to charge the president with abuse of power (withholding arms shipments to Ukraine in exchange for a personal favor) and obstruction of Congress (refusal to answer congressional subpoenas and provide documents legally sought under the authority of congressional investigation). He was never charged with obstruction of justice. At the end of the impeachment hearings/trial, Congress voted along strict party lines, with a unanimous Republican vote in the House and only one dissenting vote in the Senate. The president's obstruction persists to this day; he continues to call proven and ongoing Russian cyber warfare against the United States a hoax.

13

FINAL THOUGHTS

THE AUTHOR OF *A WARNING* by Anonymous (a senior Trump administration official) ends the book with the story of Flight 93, which crashed in an open field in Pennsylvania on September 11, 2001; and highlights the bravery and action of the passengers who decided to rush the cockpit and overpower the hijackers. The author pays tribute to Todd Beamer, an account manager, whose leadership in the moment led to that decision and his now famous last words, "Let's roll." American history is filled with many such heroes.

Both my parents served in WWII, my two older brothers served in Vietnam and I served in Afghanistan. We all witnessed tremendous sacrifices for this country. My father-in-law was shot three times by a Japanese Zero and miraculously survived. His younger brother, John, was killed on Iwo Jima, strafed across the abdomen by machine gun fire. I often think of him in the landing craft going toward that beach and the commitment that he and so many others were willing to make, to pay the ultimate sacrifice for their country and for freedom. Then I think of the many members of our present Congress who are thus far unwilling to even risk reelection. I hope that some, or many, have a change of heart/conscience and muster enough courage to act selflessly on behalf of our democracy before it's too late.

NOTES

Page 4 The president initially announced "I had to fire General Flynn because he lied to the Vice President and the FBI..." (Twitter 12/2/17). Officially he was allowed to resign.

Page 18 Iran Nuclear Agreement (In 2015 Iran agreed to a long-term deal on its nuclear program with a group of world powers known as the P5+1—the U.S., UK, France, China, Russia and Germany. Under the accord, Iran agreed to limit its sensitive activities and allow in international inspectors in return for lifting of crippling economic sanctions).

Page 20 The Group of Eight (G8) refers to the group of eight highly industrialized nations—France, Germany, Italy, the United Kingdom, Japan, the United States, Canada, and Russia—that hold an annual meeting to foster consensus on global issues like economic growth and crisis management, global security, energy, and terrorism.

Page 20 During the Cuban Missile Crisis, leaders of the U.S. and the Soviet Union engaged in a tense, 13-day political and military standoff in October 1962 over the installation of nuclear-armed Soviet missiles in Cuba, just 90 miles from U.S. shores. Disaster was avoided when the U.S. agreed to Soviet leader Nikita Khrushchev's offer to remove the Cuban missiles in exchange for the U.S. promising not to invade Cuba. Kennedy also secretly agreed to remove U.S. missiles from Turkey.

Page 24 The United Nations Commission on Human Rights was established in 1946 to weave the international fabric that protects our fundamental rights and freedoms. It also acted as a forum where countries large or small, nongovernmental groups and human rights defenders from around the world voiced their concerns.

Page 24 The president and his lawyer, Rudy Giuliani, launched a campaign to put pressure on the Ukrainian president, Volodymyr Zelensky, to investigate former Vice President Joe Biden and his son, Hunter, for possible corruption. Joe Biden was the likely Democratic opponent in the 2020 election. One result from the impeachment hearings was the finding that the president engaged in a quid pro quo: the release of U.S. arms to Ukraine for a public announcement of an investigation of Biden.

Page 25 On October 25, 2017, Senator Jeff Flake gave a speech to his Senate colleagues and said that we must never accept that which is obviously abnormal as a new normal, that we must never accept the daily sundering of our democratic principles, the flagrant disregard for truth and decency, or labeling things that threaten our Republic, as politics. He told them that he was witnessing something dangerous to democracy. He said our strength comes from our values and when our children ask us in the future, "Why didn't we do something?" We must think how we are going to answer that. He said, "Enough is enough!" He said that we must return to James Madison's separation of powers. Decency must not fail to call out indecency. If we remain silent due to political considerations at the expense of liberty we forsake our obligations. He reminded them this is a matter of duty and conscience, to do otherwise was moral treason. "When we have been at our most prosperous it was when we were most principled." He concluded by saying values are what are indispensible and our duty is to preserve them.

Page 25 The Pentagon Papers was the name given to a top-secret Department of Defense study of U.S. political and military involvement in Vietnam from 1945 to 1967. A copy of the classified study were leaked by a military analyst, Daniel Ellsberg, to the *New York Times*.

Page 25 In June 1972 a break-in to the Democratic National Committee headquarters, located in the Watergate Complex of buildings in Foggy Bottom, Washington, D.C., led to an investigation that revealed multiple abuses of power by the Nixon administration. the *Washington Post* broke the story and two *Post* reporters, Bob Woodward and Carl Bernstein, uncovered most of the details of the Watergate scandal.

Page 25 The Supreme Court ruled that the Commerce Department's decision to add a citizenship question to the 2020 census violated federal law. The opinion delivered a setback to the Trump administration's last-minute attempt to add an untested citizenship question to the census.

Page 26 The Army-McCarthy hearings were a series of hearings held by the U.S. Senate's Subcommittee on Investigations to investigate conflicting accusations between the U.S. Army and U.S. Senator Joseph McCarthy, Republican, Wisconsin, who said the Army was infiltrated with Communists.

Page 26 Brexit is the withdrawal of the United Kingdom (UK) from the European Union (EU), following a UK-wide referendum in June 2016.

Page 28 The North Atlantic Treaty Organization (NATO) is an intergovernmental military alliance between 30 North American and European countries. Its main purpose, in its inception, was to defend each other from the possibility of Communist Soviet Union taking control of their nation.

Page 31 Gaslighting is a form of psychological manipulation in which a person or a group covertly sows seeds of doubt in a targeted individual, making them question their own memory, perception, or judgment, often evoking in them a cognitive dissonance and other changes such as low self-esteem.

Page 35 The Fifth and Fourteenth Amendments to the U.S. Constitution both contain a "due process" clause dealing with the administration of justice. Due process acts as a safeguard from arbitrary denial of life, liberty, or property by the government outside the sanctions of law.

Page 35 Radio Sputnik was created by Vladimir Putin to advance Russian interests abroad. Sputnik operates radio stations in Washington D.C., and Kansas City, Missouri; it is owned and operated by the Russian government.

Page 43 WikiLeaks is an international non-profit organization that publishes news leaks and classified media provided by anonymous sources.

Page 43 The G20 (or Group of Twenty) is an international forum for the governments and central bank governors from 19 countries and the European Union.

Page 49 The president was interviewed by conservative FOX TV host, Bill O'Reilly, February 5, 2017.

Page 59 Britain First is a far-right, British fascist political organization formed in 2011 by former members of the British National Party (BNP).

Page 66 *The Bachelor* is an American dating and relationship reality television series.

Nolan with Ground Assault Convoy, Khoyr Kot Castle, 2007

STEVE NOLAN lives in Newtown, Pennsylvania. His poems were featured on National Public Radio's *Morning Edition* (September 24, 2007) upon his return from Afghanistan, in a story called, "Mother, Son Share Experiences of War." He is the author of *Notes from Afghanistan; Go Deep*, a collaboration with the artist NJ DeVico; and *Base Camp*.

Printed in the USA
CPSIA information can be obtained
at www.ICGtesting.com
JSHW020008290923
49034JS00006B/23

9 781933 974408